THE ELECTRIC LIGHT

THOMAS EDISON'S ILLUMINATING INVENTION

MILESTONES
IN AMERICAN HISTORY

MILESTONES
IN
AMERICAN HISTORY

THE ELECTRIC LIGHT

THOMAS EDISON'S ILLUMINATING INVENTION

LIZ SONNEBORN

CHELSEA HOUSE
PUBLISHERS

An imprint of Infobase Publishing

The Electric Light: Thomas Edison's Illuminating Invention

Chelsea House
An imprint of Infobase Publishing
132 West 31st Street
New York, NY 10001

ISBN-10: 0-7910-9350-6
ISBN-13: 978-0-7910-9350-4

Library of Congress Cataloging-in-Publication Data
Sonneborn, Liz.
  The electric light : Thomas Edison's illuminating invention / Liz Sonneborn.
     p. cm. — (Milestones in American history)
  Includes bibliographical references and index.
  ISBN 0-7910-9350-6 (hardcover)
  1. Edison, Thomas A. (Thomas Alva), 1847–1931—Juvenile literature.
[1. Electric lighting—Juvenile literature.] I. Title. II. Series.

  TK4351.S65 2007
  621.3092—dc22   2006034432

Text design by Erik Lindstrom
Cover design by Ben Peterson

Printed in the United States of America

Bang FOF 10 9 8 7 6 5 4 3 2 1

This book is printed on acid-free paper.

CONTENTS

Edison's Newest Marvel

On a pleasant Saturday in mid-September 1878, a reporter for the *New York Sun* took a trip from bustling New York City to the small farming village of Menlo Park, New Jersey. After hopping a ferry and a train, he traveled up a dirt road from the train station until he spied a large two-story clapboard structure. The unimpressive building was the home of America's first invention factory. Inside was the most famous inventor in the United States—Thomas Edison.

Edison, at the time only 31 years old, had come to Menlo Park two years before. By that time, he was already a successful inventor, known particularly for his improvements to electric telegraph systems. Looking for a quiet place where his creative instincts could flourish, he poured his newfound fortune into his New Jersey laboratory and hired a team of top-notch engineers, scientists, and machinists.

When Thomas Edison was 30 years old, he invented the phonograph, which he called the "talking machine." Although Edison did not earn financial stability from his invention, he did gain respect and was tabbed the "Wizard of Menlo Park" by the press. Edison is pictured here demonstrating his tinfoil phonograph at the White House on April 18, 1878.

Their greatest triumph so far was a simple phonograph, which they developed by accident while working on how to make the sound volume on a telephone louder. Much to Edison's disappointment, he could not figure out a way to make the "talking machine" a commercial success. The public and the press marveled at the device, which could make a crude recording of the human voice on a cylinder made of tinfoil. But the phonograph was expensive, so Edison failed to find many customers for his invention.

Still, the phonograph brought him something nearly as valuable as money—publicity. Edison spent the early months of 1878 traveling and demonstrating his technological marvel. The exciting (though, to Edison, financially worthless) device earned him a new nickname in the press: "the Wizard of Menlo Park." This wizard, newspapers suggested, could do anything he set his mind to. In fact, when the *Daily Graphic* published an April Fool's Day story titled "Edison Invents a Machine that Will Feed the Human Race," other newspapers reprinted the story, mistakenly presenting the joke as fact.

A BOLD ANNOUNCEMENT

Given Edison's reputation, the *New York Sun* reporter was happy to pay the famous inventor a visit. Edison had a showman's instinct and a gift for turning a clever phrase, so the reporter was sure to come away with some interesting quotes. But he was not prepared for what Edison had in store for him. The inventor took the opportunity to announce to the reporter, and therefore to the world, that he was ready to embark on his most ambitious project yet.

The reporter's article ran on September 16, 1878, in the *Sun*'s Monday edition, with a headline that trumpeted Edison's latest scheme—"Edison's Newest Marvel. Sending Cheap Light, Heat, and Power by Electricity." In the article, the reporter explained, "Mr. Edison says that he has discovered how to make electricity a cheap and practicable substitute for illuminating gas."[1] Although "many scientific men have worked assiduously in that direction, but with little success," Edison was confident he would "solve the difficult problem . . . within a few days."[2]

The great inventor was a bit vague on details, fearful that these other scientists might steal his ideas. But he was hardly shy about heralding the brilliance of his recent discoveries. "I have it now!" he declared to the reporter, adding, "and, singularly enough, I have obtained it through an entirely different process than that from which scientific men have ever sought to secure it. They have all been working in the same groove, and when it is known how I have accomplished my object, everybody will wonder why they have never thought of it, it is so simple."[3]

Edison's promises did not stop there. He boldly announced, "With the process I have just discovered, I can produce a thousand—aye, ten thousand—[lights] from one machine. Indeed, the number may be said to be infinite. When the brilliancy and cheapness of the lights are made known to the public—which will be in a few weeks, or just as soon as I can thoroughly protect the process—illumination by carbureted hydrogen gas will be discarded."[4]

LIGHTING WITH GAS

When Edison was making his declaration, most Americans still lived in rural areas. They lit their houses and businesses with the same devices that had been used for generations—candles and lamps fueled by kerosene or whale oil. But increasingly, Americans were moving to urban areas. By the 1870s, many city homes, businesses, shops, factories, and streets were illuminated by gas lamps. The gas was sent to streetlights through underground pipes below streets. Pipes were also installed in the walls of buildings to carry gas to wall lamps. When the sun went down, people turned on the gas and lit these lamps by hand.

Gaslights were certainly a vast improvement over candles. They cast a glow of light over city streets and building interiors, allowing people to work or indulge in leisure activities well into the night. British writer Robert Louis Stevenson celebrated the wonders of gas lighting: "Mankind and its supper parties were no longer at the mercy of a few miles of sea-fog; sundown no longer emptied the promenade; and the day was lengthened out to every man's fancy. The city folk had stars of their own; biddable, domesticated stars."[5]

But gaslights had plenty of disadvantages. The flame that produced the light was always flickering and giving off smoke. Over time, the fumes from the lamps blackened walls, curtains, and furniture. Far worse, they could sometimes catch a building on fire or even explode. The lights also released ammonia, sulfur, and carbon dioxide, often enough to make people dizzy or give them headaches. And in the event of a silent, odorless gas leak, these chemicals would escape into the air, sometimes proving deadly.

THE ARC LIGHT

As the *New York Sun* reporter noted, scientists had been trying for years to come up with an electric alternative to the gaslight. But harnessing electricity's powers had proven frustrating. Although electricity was first studied by the ancient Greeks, by Edison's day, it still had relatively few practical applications. The great exceptions were the telegraph, invented by Samuel Morse in 1837, and telephone, patented by Alexander Graham Bell in 1876.

A practical and inexpensive electric light, however, remained just out of reach for scientists. The closest thing was the arc light. The first arc light was demonstrated by British scientist Sir Humphry Davy in 1809. Before an audience at London's Royal Institution, Davy attached a battery to two charcoal rods with a small gap between them. As the electricity flowed between the two charcoal conductors, an arc of light appeared in the gap.

Davy's gadget was far from practical for everyday use. Battery power was expensive, and his carbon sticks quickly burned up under the light's intense heat. By the late 1870s, however, several European scientists made some crucial improvements. Their arc lights ran on powerful electric generators and were fitted with a series of carbon rods, allowing them to burn for as many as 16 hours. By 1878, several outdoor areas in Paris were illuminated at night with arc lights.

But, like gaslights, even these improved arc lights had their problems. They sent off a steady stream of very strong light—so strong they could only be used in large spaces, such as city squares and huge factories. The lights also had to be erected on high poles above eye level, or they would hurt people's eyes. They required a good deal of maintenance, and even when they were kept up well, they often sent off a frightening barrage of sparks.

A DEMONSTRATION IN ANSONIA

Like most inventors knowledgeable in electricity, Edison had toyed around with creating a better electric light. But it was only when he saw an arc light with his own eyes that he became truly excited by the project.

It was about a week before he met with the *Sun* reporter. Edison accompanied his friend George Barker, a University of Pennsylvania professor, to Ansonia, Connecticut. Barker wanted Edison to meet William Wallace, the owner of a brass and copper factory there. Wallace had been studying electricity for a decade and had created an electric generator that he called a *telemachon*. Reporter Charles Dana accompanied Edison and Barker, and later wrote about what happened.

Delighted to meet the famous inventor, Wallace proudly showed Edison what his telemachon could do. The generator was wired up to a row of eight arc lights. Once the generator let loose an electric current, the bright lights lit up the sky. Dana described Edison's enthusiastic response: "Edison was enraptured. He fairly gloated over it. . . . He ran from the instruments to the lights, and from the lights back to the instruments. He sprawled over a table with the SIMPLICITY OF A CHILD, and made all kinds of calculations."[6]

Within moments, Edison told Wallace, "I believe I can beat you making the electric light. I do not think you are working in the right direction."[7] Wallace graciously shook the younger man's hand, accepting his challenge.

A PROMISING START

For Edison, the time was right to take on something new and something big. The employees and equipment needed to keep the Menlo Park lab running were expensive. Edison required a steady stream of income, which his phonograph had not provided. Working on improving the telephone had seemed like a promising venture, but the field was already crowded with inventors working furiously to make their mark. In contrast, few people were involved with electric lighting. If Edison were to make a breakthrough, he would have the field virtually to himself. He would surely make a fortune, maybe enough to run Menlo Park for the rest of his life.

Edison was inspired by Wallace's generator, which, unlike a battery, could create plenty of inexpensive electrical energy. He saw in an instant that if he could figure out a way to connect it to many smaller lights, he could create a workable, inexpensive electrical lighting system. About a month after the visit, he told a reporter about his revelation:

> [In Ansonia], I saw for the first time everything in practical operation. It was all before me. I saw the thing had not gone so far but that I had a chance. I saw that what had been done had never been made practically useful. The intense light had not been subdivided so that it could be brought into private houses.[8]

Rushing back to Menlo Park, Edison began to work. His early calculations and drawings only made him more confident that he was on the verge of a great discovery. He

After visiting the inventor William Wallace at his home in Connecticut in 1878, Thomas Edison was inspired to find a way to generate electric light. Within a week of his return to his laboratory in Menlo Park, New Jersey, he confidently predicted that he would bring light and heat to people's homes. One of Edison's early technical drawings for his planned lightbulb is pictured here.

was so sure in fact that after only a week of work, he was willing to brag to the *New York Sun* reporter that he would not only bring electric light into people's homes, but that he would bring electric power and heat as well. The *Sun* reported: "[T]he same wire that brings the light to you," Mr. Edison continued, "will also bring power and heat. With the power you can run an elevator, a sewing machine or any other mechanical contrivance that requires a motor, and by means of the heat you may cook your food. To utilize the heat, it will duly be necessary to have the ovens or stoves properly arranged for its reception. This can be done at trifling cost."[9]

But Edison's biggest boast appeared at the end of the article. Undoubtedly egged on by Edison, the reporter concluded it with, "Edison will soon give a public exhibition of his new invention."[10]

CHALLENGES AHEAD

The *Sun*'s article immediately caused a stir. It was reprinted in newspapers in Philadelphia, Chicago, and other cities. But it had its biggest impact in New York City, or more specifically, in the financial center of Wall Street. Edison's friend and lawyer Grosvenor P. Lowrey had no trouble lining up investors for the inventor's new business, the Edison Electric Light Company. While the company's stock sold out, prices for shares in gas lighting companies plummeted. It was a testament to Wall Street investors' faith that Edison would soon put the gas companies out of business.

Not everyone was so excited. Edison had many detractors in the scientific community who dismissed his claims as nothing but hot air. As English electrician John T. Sprague wrote, "Neither Mr. Edison nor anyone else can override the well-known laws of Nature, and when he is made to say that the same wire which brings you light will also bring you power and heat, there is no difficulty in seeing that more is promised than can possibly be performed. The talk about cooking food by heat derived by electricity is absurd."[11]

Edison ignored the criticism, completely convinced he would see a breakthrough within weeks, if not days. But the confident Edison could not have imagined he was only at the beginning of his 14-year struggle to bring the electric light to the world. And along the way, he would be forced to overcome an array of challenges, including technical obstacles, economic limitations, ferocious competitors, and even his own ego.

Ambition
and Invention

O n February 11, 1847, Thomas Alva Edison was born during a snowy winter night at his family's home in Milan, Ohio. Nicknamed Al, he was the seventh and last child of Samuel and Nancy Edison. The three Edison children closest to Thomas's age all died in early childhood. With his three surviving siblings already teenagers, he grew up much like an only child, with plenty of attention from his doting parents.

In Thomas's early years, Milan was a small, but growing center for trade. However, when railroads were built to other nearby towns, but not to Milan, its trade industry faltered. Likely seeking better business opportunities, the Edisons moved to Port Huron, Michigan, when Al was seven.

GROWING UP

Port Huron was a large town with a booming lumber industry. Samuel Edison moved his family into a big two-story home known as the White House by locals. He built a 100-foot observation tower next to the house, and for 25 cents, visitors could climb the tower and see a beautiful view of Lake Huron.

The tower was just one of Samuel Edison's many businesses. At various times, he ran a grocery store, operated a farm, sold timber, and dabbled in real estate. Despite his energy and enterprise, the family was often in financial trouble. They sometimes rented out rooms of their house to other people, just to make ends meet.

Soon after arriving in town, Thomas Edison's mother enrolled him in a one-room school. Thomas was a poor student, ridiculed by his teacher for being inattentive in class. As he later recounted, "One day, I heard the teacher tell the visiting school inspector that I was addled and it would not be worthwhile keeping me in school any longer. I was so hurt by this last straw that I burst out crying and went home and told my mother about it."[12] Nancy Edison took him out of the school, ending his three months of formal education. She probably wanted to protect her son, who was physically weak and often sick, but the Edisons no doubt were also happy to save on school fees by teaching the boy at home.

As a former schoolteacher, Thomas's mother probably taught him using the standard readers and textbooks of the day. But his father's library played a far greater role in his education. The inventor once explained, "My mother taught me how to read good books quickly and correctly, and this opened up a great world in literature."[13] He soon developed a love of reading, which would remain with him for the rest of his life. By 13, he was reading sophisticated works of history and philosophy, including David Hume's *History of England* and Edward Gibbon's *Decline and Fall of the Roman Empire*.

A FASCINATION WITH TECHNOLOGY

Among his favorite books was *A School Compendium of Natural and Experimental Philosophy* by R. G. Parker. The book had detailed illustrations and instructions for experimenting with batteries and electricity. It also had a chart of the Morse code alphabet, a communication system invented by Samuel Morse for sending messages over a telegraph.

The telegraph, invented in 1837, was only 10 years older than Thomas Edison. But by the time he was in his early teens, the telegraph had already drastically changed American life. Before the telegraph, letters and other forms of communication had to be physically carried from the sender to the recipient, often taking days, weeks, or even months, depending on the distance between them. In contrast, a message sent by telegraph could reach its destination, no matter how far away it was, in a matter of seconds.

In a telegraph system, the telegraphic devices of the sender and the receiver were connected by a series of wires. By pressing down a key, the sender sent electronic impulses through the wires. The receiver's device then recorded these impulses as indentions on a strip of paper. The messages were sent in Morse code, which assigned a unique pattern of short and long impulses to each letter of the alphabet. Short impulses were called "dots" and long ones were called "dashes."

Thomas was fascinated by telegraphy. He taught himself Morse code and built a simple telegraph system that connected his house with a friend's house about half a mile away. He also toyed with a handmade steam engine railroad, which he built in a room in his home. It was a project that reflected another of his boyhood obsessions—the railroad.

RIDING THE RAILS

When Thomas was 12, the Grand Trunk Railroad of Canada built a train depot within walking distance of his house. Port Huron passengers on the new rail line could reach the city of Detroit, Michigan, in just three hours.

Like many boys of the era, Thomas dreamed of one day becoming a train engineer. With his father's help, he landed

While Thomas Edison was growing up, he became fascinated with trains and hoped one day to become an engineer. Edison is pictured here at the age of 12, around the time his father persuaded the Grand Trunk Railroad to hire him as a newsboy.

a job that must have seemed to him to be the next best thing. He was hired as a newsboy on the Detroit line. The train left for Detroit at seven o'clock in the morning, and after a long layover, returned to Port Huron at nine o'clock at night. While the train was running, Thomas carried a large tray through the aisles of the passenger cars. The tray was stocked with newspapers, magazines, candy, peanuts, sandwiches, and anything else Thomas could persuade passengers to buy on their trip.

The job was a great way for a clever and ambitious teenager to make money. Thomas quickly learned to be a good salesman. He was successful enough that he eventually hired a few other boys as helpers to expand his business. Thomas also started several side businesses to increase his income. For instance, he bought high-quality produce in Detroit, and then resold it in Port Huron, jacking up the price and taking home a healthy profit.

To further increase his take, Thomas started publishing his own newspaper. Every time he sold other papers, he got a small commission. But every time he sold his own, he got to pocket the entire sales price. For six months in 1862, he put out the *Weekly Herald*, printing it in a baggage storeroom on the train. The newspaper published rail schedules, articles about the railroad and its employees, price lists of farm products, birth and death announcements, and plenty of local gossip. He eventually sold 500 subscriptions, while also routinely selling hundreds of more copies on the train.

LEARNING ABOUT ELECTRICITY

As busy as he was with his businesses, Thomas found time for his other interests. On his layovers in Detroit, he spent hours in the city library, reading about any topic that interested him. It was there that he discovered the works of Michael Faraday, a British scientist who once worked as an assistant to Sir Humphry Davy, the inventor of the arc light. In the early nineteenth century, Faraday demonstrated the interconnections between chemistry, electricity, and magnetism. Reading Faraday's *Experimental Researches in Electricity and Magnetism*

(continues on page 18)

MICHAEL FARADAY
(1791–1867)

A Pioneer in the Sciences
of Electricity and Magnetism

Through his pioneering work in electromagnetism, experimental scientist Michael Faraday helped usher in the modern electronic age. The son of a blacksmith, he was born in Surrey, England, on September 22, 1791. Because of his father's chronically ill health, his family was very poor.

When he was 14, Faraday had to leave school after learning only the basics of reading, writing, and arithmetic. He was apprenticed for seven years to a bookbinder. While working, Faraday would often read the books he was binding. He discovered that despite his meager education, he was capable of understanding complex subjects. Faraday read the entire *Encyclopaedia Britannica*. The entry on electricity especially intrigued him. He began reading everything he could find on the subject and set up a small laboratory in his room to perform experiments. A customer at the shop gave Faraday tickets to a series of lectures by the famous scientist Sir Humphry Davy. Davy was a professor at the Royal Institution of London, a leading scientific organization devoted to educating the public about advances in science. During Davy's lectures, Faraday took detailed notes. He also drew illustrations of the devices Davy demonstrated.

When Faraday's apprenticeship came to an end, he decided to become a scientist—an unusual ambition for someone with so little education. As Faraday once wrote, "[My] desire to escape from trade, which I thought vicious and selfish, and to enter into the services of Science . . . induced me at last to take the bold and simple step of writing to Sir H. Davy."* In his letter, he included copies of his lecture notes and illustrations. Davy was so impressed by

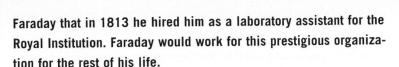

Faraday that in 1813 he hired him as a laboratory assistant for the Royal Institution. Faraday would work for this prestigious organization for the rest of his life.

Becoming the director of the laboratory in 1825, Faraday frequently gave lectures to the public. But Faraday's greatest contribution to the world of science came from his laboratory experiments. In 1821, Danish physicist Hans Christian Øersted showed that an electrical current could move a compass needle, which suggested a close connection between electricity and magnetism. Fascinated by Øersted's work, Faraday launched a series of experiments that eventually proved that magnetism and electricity were different expressions of the same force—the electromagnetic force.

Through his work, Faraday created a device that could convert electrical energy into mechanical movement, thereby inventing the electric motor. He also found that by moving a magnet through a coil of wire, he could produce electrical energy. This discovery was the birth of the electrical generator. Faraday was motivated by a sheer love of knowledge. His work, however, proved to have tremendous practical applications. The electrical generator made it possible to create electrical energy, while the electrical motor allowed humankind to put this energy to use.

By the 1840s, Faraday was too sickly to conduct laboratory work, although he continued to teach and give lectures. He also devoted his later years to writing the three-volume *Experimental Researches in Electricity and Magnetism*. He died on August 25, 1867, at the age of 75.

---

* Jill Jonnes, *Empires of Light: Edison, Tesla, Westinghouse, and the Race to Electrify the World* (New York: Random House, 2003), 38.

(continued from page 15)

not only gave Thomas a better understanding of the field of electromagnetism—it also provided him with a role model. Like Thomas, Faraday had come from a modest background. He was the lowly son of a blacksmith, but through determination and talent, Faraday emerged as one of the leading scientists of his day.

While riding the rails, Thomas also conducted experiments in a baggage storeroom. He kept vials of chemicals and other equipment next to his printing press. But after he accidentally set the room on fire during an experiment, the railroad closed his laboratory. He set it up again in the basement of his family's home.

Edison later claimed that a conductor slapped him on his ears as punishment for the fire. This was just one of several explanations Edison gave for his loss of hearing, which grew worse throughout his lifetime. Even as a teenager, he was fairly deaf. However, his deafness had one benefit: it helped him tune out the world and concentrate on his studies and experiments.

STUDYING TELEGRAPHY

By the fall of 1862, Thomas was focusing his attention on telegraphy. At the time, the United States was embroiled in the Civil War (1861–1865). The country had recruited nearly all experienced telegraph operators to work for the military. Businesses lost their operators as a result, and so were willing to hire self-taught young men, like Thomas, as replacements.

Among the companies looking for operators were railroads. They used telegraphic messages to communicate any delays from station to station, which helped cut down on train collisions. Thomas became friends with J. U. MacKenzie, a stationmaster who let him listen in on the telegraphic transmissions. According to early Edison biographies, MacKenzie felt indebted to Thomas after the young man saved MacKenzie's three-year-old son, who had wandered in front of an oncoming

Fifteen-year-old Thomas Edison is depicted in this engraving saving three-year-old Jimmie MacKenzie from being hit by a train. Jimmie was the son of J. U. MacKenzie, the stationmaster at the Mount Clemens, Michigan, train station. Although Edison most likely made up the story, the elder MacKenzie quickly struck up a friendship with him and helped train him to be a telegraph operator.

train. Whether out of gratitude or just kindness, MacKenzie took Thomas under his wing and helped train him to become an operator. For 18 hours a day, Thomas practiced sending and receiving messages, hoping to become skilled enough to land a job.

In 1863, Thomas was hired to work the night shift on the Grand Trunk line from Stratford Junction, New Hampshire, to Toronto, Ontario, in Canada. It was the beginning of his adventure as a "tramp" telegrapher, traveling from town to town and city to city. Symbolic of the big change in his life, Thomas discarded his old childhood nickname "Al," telling people to instead call him "Tom."

A TELEGRAPHER'S TRAVELS

Working as a telegrapher, Thomas traveled throughout the Midwest. For the first time in his life, he got a sense of the world outside of Michigan. He also found a circle of friends among his fellow operators, many of whom shared his interests. Like him, most were fascinated by technology, science, and most of all, telegraphy. They all wanted to become the fastest operators they could be. The faster they were, the better the jobs they could get. The biggest prize of all was working for a news service. Landing that kind of job brought a high salary, not to mention the envy of everyone else in the field.

The young telegraph operators were highly competitive, often holding informal contests to show off their skills. Experienced telegraphers also liked to play pranks on new recruits. But generally, Thomas found many supportive friends within the telegraphy community. Many operators were adolescents who were away from home for the first time. They leaned on each other for emotional support and frequently helped one another find jobs. That was particularly important for Thomas, who seemed to have a knack for getting fired. But losing one job mattered little when he could just get on the telegraph and ask friends hundreds of miles away for information on any new openings.

AN INSPIRED INVENTION

Thomas found this world exciting and stimulating. It also sparked his fierce ambition. He was determined to land a news job. On his off hours, he would practice copying down press stories coming through the wire. Instead of translating the messages from the paper strips indented with telegraphic code, he and his fellow telegraphers listened to the telegraph register's "sounder," which made a clicking noise—a short click for a dot, a long one for a dash. While listening, the operators wrote down the corresponding letters by hand.

In 1864, while he was in Indianapolis, Indiana, Thomas became frustrated with his progress. He had trouble writing fast and legibly at the rate the messages came in, about 40 words per minute. Frustrated that he was too slow even with all his practicing, he decided to find a way around the problem. Using pieces from several discarded telegraph registers, he crafted a new device. When he fed a paper tape with an indented message through it, it made the corresponding clicks at a slower rate, about 25 words per minute. He found that at that speed, he could take down the message in very legible type and with almost no mistakes.

Thomas's years in telegraphy were invaluable to his later career. He saw many new places, learned to work with other people, and became familiar with a wide range of different companies and business practices. Listening on the news wires, he gained an appreciation of the potential and power of the press. Most of all, he discovered how his flair for invention could solve practical problems. His Indianapolis invention was his first, but it would hardly be his last.

The Wizard

When Thomas Edison was 20, he received a telegraph message from a friend telling him there was an opening at the Western Union bureau in Boston, Massachusetts. Edison headed east for the Boston job, which soon led to an even better post—the nightshift at the most prestigious press wire in New York City. Edison preferred the night shift, because it left his days largely free for reading and experiments. His lowest priority was sleep. He had taught himself how to get by with only four or five hours a night, along with a few catnaps here and there during the day.

Edison began keeping detailed notes about his personal work. He also frequently wrote about what he was doing in magazine articles for *The Telegrapher* and the *Journal of the Telegraph*. His writings made his name familiar to telegraphers throughout the country.

In one brief notice published in *The Telegrapher*, Edison proudly announced a big change in his life. He wrote that he was quitting his job with Western Union. Edison wanted to devote all his time "to bringing out his inventions."[14]

THE FIRST PATENT

Edison took this bold step after applying for his first patent with the U.S. government. A patent grants an inventor the exclusive rights to make and sell a device for a specific period of time. Like all inventors, Edison knew that in order to make a living, he had to get a patent on any worthwhile invention he came up with.

His first patented invention was an electronic vote recorder. Edison had hoped legislatures would want to use his voting system, but to his disappointment, he had trouble finding buyers. The invention could only be seen as a financial failure. But even then, Edison recognized that failure was an essential part of his work: Only by learning what would not work could he anticipate what *would* work. Instead of being discouraged, he took heart from his vote recorder. In Edison's eyes, his first patent was evidence that he had the ability to take on the risky job of inventing.

In his early years as an inventor, Edison decided to stick with the field he knew best—telegraphy. He started a service for businesses that sent them stock prices by telegraph. His service soon had 25 subscribers. Edison invested nearly every penny he earned into experimenting with new telegraphic devices. For a time, he tried to create a telegraph receiver that would type out messages in letters, so people could read messages hot off the wire without knowing Morse code. He also sought investors for a duplex telegraph line—one that would send transmissions in both directions—between the cities of Rochester and New York.

ON HIS OWN

When none of his ideas quite panned out, he took a job as superintendent of the Gold & Stock Reporting Telegraph

One of Thomas Edison's first inventions was a stock ticker called the "Universal Stock Printer," which he patented in 1869. This stock ticker, as well as other inventions made for stockbrokers, earned Edison $40,000, which he used to finance a laboratory in Newark, New Jersey.

Company. The firm sent price quotes on gold and stocks to bankers and brokers around New York City. But soon, he once again decided to strike out on his own. With Franklin Pope, the former superintendent of Gold & Stock, he formed Pope, Edison & Company. Edison and Pope set themselves up to compete with their old employer.

The partnership did not last long. When Gold & Stock offered Edison financial backing to come up with a speedier automatic telegraph, he dissolved his working relationship with Pope. Edison then set up shop in Newark, New Jersey, calling his new company the Newark Telegraph Works. Before long, Edison had approximately 50 people working for him. Among them was

16-year-old Mary Stillwell. After a three-month courtship, she and Edison married on Christmas Day of 1871.

Even after his marriage, Edison spent little time at home. He was a compulsive worker, devoting most of his waking hours to tinkering with new ideas. At his side was Charles Batchelor, a quiet Englishman whom Edison hired as his right-hand man. Whenever inspiration struck, Edison would hurriedly jot down notes and scrawl out pictures of new devices. The highly organized Batchelor would then help develop these raw ideas into workable machines. Batchelor once described their working methods: "We work all night experimenting and sleep till noon in the day. We have got 54 different things on the carpet & some we have been on for 4 or 5 years. Edison is an indefatigable worker & there is no kind of failure however disastrous affects him."[15]

With Batchelor, Edison continued to work hard on coming up with improved telegraphic equipment. In 1875, he had his biggest success to date when financier Jay Gould, president of Atlantic and Pacific Telegraph, paid him $30,000 for the rights to one device. Edison wrote, with some understatement, that it was "somewhat more than I thought I could get."[16]

MOVING TO MENLO PARK

As usual, Edison poured the money he made back into his business. He decided to set up a bigger and better working facility in Menlo Park, New Jersey. There would be little to distract him and his workers in this small, quiet village, yet it was only a short train trip away from New York City. Isolated but not too isolated, Menlo Park seemed to offer the best of both worlds, making it an ideal location for Edison's new invention factory.

Construction on the facility was completed in early 1876. It was a huge, rectangular two-story building, 100 feet long and 30 feet wide, with a balcony overlooking a cow pasture. Downstairs was a machine shop, where machinists crafted

In early 1876, Thomas Edison moved into his new industrial research lab in Menlo Park, New Jersey, the exterior of which is pictured here. Edison's lab was the first institution set up for the express purpose of producing technological innovations and scientific research.

models of Edison's ideas. The building also housed a steam engine, which powered the generators used to create electrical current for Edison's experiments.

Upstairs, the space was filled with worktables covered with batteries and electrical devices in all stages of construction. From floor to ceiling, the walls were lined with shelves holding more than 2,500 bottles filled with just about every known chemical substance. One reporter called the work area "a wilderness of wires, jars of vitroil [sulfuric acid], strips of tin foil, old clay pipes, copies of the great daily newspapers, and sundry bits of machinery of unknown power."[17]

Off to the side was Edison's own small worktable. He usually wandered throughout the workroom, keeping an eye on what everyone was doing. But sometimes he retreated to his worktable, taking a moment alone to write down notes on his latest thoughts. Occasionally, he disappeared downstairs to a hidden cabinet he could crawl into for a quick nap.

The most important feature of Menlo Park was its staff. Edison's employees included chemists, machinists, laboratory technicians, bookkeepers, and secretaries. But he relied most on a handful of inventors and scientists devoted to realizing his vision. Edison demanded a great deal from them. They worked long hours every day, taking time off only for quick meals and a little sleep at a boardinghouse near the laboratory. Most of these workers were extremely devoted to Edison. They admired the inventor, who in turn treated them with respect and listened to their ideas. Edison's men were also confident that if their ideas panned out, their employer would compensate them well.

By setting up such an elaborate shop at Menlo Park, Edison hoped to send a message to the press and the public that he was in the inventing business for the long haul. More significantly, he built the perfect environment there to unleash his creativity, giving him a huge advantage over his competitors. As Edison scholars Robert Friedel and Paul Israel have explained, "No other inventor in the nineteenth century had at his disposal what Edison had—a team of skilled and intelligent co-workers armed with every instrument, tool, or material they required and dedicated to the accomplishment of whatever end Edison set out for them."[18]

NEW INVENTIONS

In March 1876, Edison was granted his first patent in more than a year. His new invention was the electric pen—a primitive version of a copying machine. As a person wrote with the pen, it made a series of tiny holes in a piece of paper, creating a stencil. The writer could then place a clean sheet under the stencil and run a roller coated with ink to make a copy of the document. Each stencil was strong enough to create about 50 copies.

Edison saw plenty of uses for the electric pen. He advertised that it could copy letters, contracts, maps, drawings, and pamphlets. Showing Edison's flair for marketing, one ad showed a picture of a kissing couple, with the caption "Like Kissing— Every Succeeding Impression is as Good as the First."[19] Priced at $35, the electric pen sold briskly.

Edison was pleased with the electric pen's success. But it provided little comfort when his rival Alexander Graham Bell announced in March 1876 that he had invented the telephone. Bell's invention was a great technological achievement that would undoubtedly reap equally huge profits.

Edison was angry that Bell had beat him to the telephone, but he still saw an opportunity to strike it big in the new telephone industry. Bell's telephone was far from perfect. It could send sound over only a short distance, and the caller had to yell into it if the receiver were to hear anything at all. Edison turned his attention to finding a way to make the sound coming through the telephone louder and clearer—an improvement that he could patent himself.

The Phonograph

Soon after starting off in this new direction, Edison once again changed course. He became intrigued by the idea that the electric impulses that sent sound over a telephone could somehow be recorded and then played back. Edison tried to record these impulses as indentions on a variety of surfaces. He had early success with a paper disc covered with wax, but he could not make a device that could use the disc to play the sound back. Even as he was struggling with his invention, word leaked out that he was on the verge of creating a "speaking telegraph." On November 17, 1877, the headline of an editorial in *Scientific American* magazine promised "A Wonderful

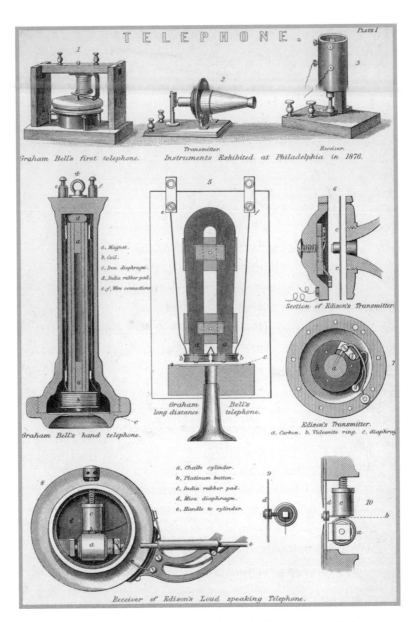

In March 1876, Alexander Graham Bell announced that he had invented the telephone. Despite being beat to the punch by Bell, Thomas Edison turned his attention to finding a way to make the sound coming from the telephone louder and clearer. Both Bell's and Edison's diagrams of telephone components are depicted in this sketch.

Invention—Speech Capable of Indefinite Repetition from Automatic Records."[20]

Less than three weeks later, the scientists at Menlo Park were playing with Edison's latest sound-recording gadget. It

"THE TALKING PHONOGRAPH"

The morning after Edison discovered his phonograph could play back sound, he packed up his machine and headed for the *Scientific American* offices in New York City. There, he gave a demonstration for the staff, including editor Alfred Beach. In the magazine's December 22, 1877, issue, Beach wrote a column titled "The Talking Phonograph," in which he described Edison's latest achievement and speculated about how the phonograph might be used in the future.

Mr. Thomas A. Edison recently came into this office, placed a little machine on our desk, turned a crank, and the machine inquired as to our health, asked how we liked the phonograph, informed us that it was very well, and bid us a cordial good night. These remarks were not only perfectly audible to ourselves, but to a dozen of more persons gathered around, and they were produced by the aid of no other mechanism than [this] simple little contrivance. . . .

No matter how familiar a person may be with modern machinery and its wonderful performances, or how clear in his mind the principle underlying this strange device may be, it is impossible to listen to the mechanical speech without his experiencing the idea that his senses are deceiving him. We have heard other talking machines. The Faber apparatus for example is a large affair as big as a parlor organ. It has a keyboard, rubber larynx and lips, and an immense amount of ingenious

was a brass cylinder fitted with a hand crank and wrapped with a sheet of tinfoil. By yelling into a mouthpiece, the operator made a dome inside the machine vibrate, which in turn caused a thin, penlike device to tap indentions into the foil. One man

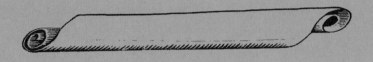

mechanism which combines to produce something like articulation in a single monotonous organ note. But here is a little affair of a few pieces of metal, set up roughly on an iron stand about a foot square, that talks in such a way, that, even if in its present imperfect form many words are not clearly distinguishable, there can be no doubt but that the inflections are those of nothing else than the human voice.

We have already pointed out the startling possibility of the voices of the dead being reheard through this device, and there is no doubt but that its capabilities are fully equal to other results just as astonishing. When it becomes possible as it doubtless will, to magnify the sound, the voices of such singers as Parepa and Titiens will not die with them, but will remain as long as the metal in which they may be embodied will last. The witness in court will find his own testimony repeated by machine confronting him on cross-examination—the testator will repeat his last will and testament into the machine so that it will be reproduced in a way that will leave no question as to his devising capacity or sanity. It is already possible by ingenious optical contrivances to throw stereoscopic photographs of people on screens in full view of an audience. Add the talking phonograph to counterfeit their voices, and it would be difficult to carry the illusion of real presence much further.*

---

*   Alfred Beach, "The Talking Photograph," *Scientific American,* December 22, 1877.

shouted "Mary had a little lamb" into the mouthpiece while another cranked the cylinder. When they tried playing back the tinfoil recording, to their amazement, they could faintly hear the nursery rhyme. The lab workers were so excited they stayed up all night, recording and playing one message after another.

Edison was delighted. He was sure that he had an invention to rival Bell's telephone in popularity. Bell agreed. Just as Edison was distraught over missing out on inventing the telephone, Bell was upset that he did not use the technology he had pioneered to invent the phonograph. He told his father-in-law that he was miserable over "let[ting] this invention slip through my fingers."[21]

Promoting His Inventions

By the spring of 1878, Edison was devoting most of his time to promoting the phonograph. He envisioned dozens of uses—from copying down speeches to singing children to sleep to recording the final words of the dying. He welcomed reporters to Menlo Park for demonstrations. They marveled at Edison's machine, which he made sing popular songs and recite Bible verses for their amusement. As part of his show, he sometimes had the phonograph interrupt him during his lecture with the words, "Oh, shut up."

During reporters' visits, Edison always took the opportunity to show them around the laboratory and explain all the other amazing inventions he was working on. When demonstrating the electric pen, he liked to write his name and the date, then run off copies for reporters to take home as souvenirs. Just as Edison hoped, the reporters inevitably wrote glowing pieces about the exciting things they had seen and heard.

Edison himself got almost as much press attention as his inventions. He was well aware that many scientists and inventors looked down on him because he had virtually no formal education. Edison tried to turn that into an advantage by presenting himself as the ultimate self-made man. During his demonstrations, he played up his humble background, wearing a wrinkled work shirt and boots instead of a suit. He also spoke in a folksy manner. Edison liked to call the phonograph his "baby," adding that he "expected it to grow up to be a big feller and support me in my old age."[22] Reporters loved the act. They lavished Edison with nicknames, calling him "The Napoleon of Invention," "The New Jersey Columbus," and most memorably, "The Wizard of Menlo Park."

The Menlo Park demonstrations were just one part of Edison's marketing campaign for the phonograph. He trained and hired agents to give demonstrations throughout the country. He published articles and letters to the editor under false names, celebrating his great invention. Edison also traveled to Washington, D.C., to give a late-night demonstration to President Rutherford B. Hayes. The president was so thrilled by the phonograph that he woke up the First Lady so she could hear it, too.

Edison's promotional campaign was a roaring success, but the excitement over the phonograph did not translate into sales. With a price tag of $100, it was little more than a very expensive plaything. It was an intriguing novelty, but one that few people could afford to buy.

A New Direction

After a few whirlwind months of promotion, Edison was not only disappointed, but also exhausted. His friend George Barker told him he needed a vacation. Barky, as the inventor called him, invited Edison to join a scientific expedition to Wyoming to watch a total eclipse of the sun.

Edison agreed to come along. During the eclipse, he wanted to test an invention called the tasimeter, which measured heat from the sun. The trip was fun and relaxing. At every train stop, young telegraphers gathered to cheer Edison, who had become a hero to them. Once out West, he visited a silver mine, saw Yellowstone National Park, and went antelope hunting. Most of all, he enjoyed talking with Barky and the other scientists. Their favorite topic was electricity and how its powers could be harnessed to help humankind.

Edison returned invigorated and inspired. Soon after, he accompanied Barky on another outing—the trip to Ansonia, Connecticut, to see William Wallace's amazing arc lights. Edison decided to put the phonograph aside for the time being. As he told a visitor, "It is a child and will grow to be a man yet; but I have a bigger thing in hand and must finish it to the temporary neglect of all other phones and graphs."[23] For almost 15 years, Edison would in fact ignore "all other phones and graphs" as he became absorbed in a single quest—the quest for a workable electric light.

Solving
the Puzzle

When Thomas Edison had announced to the *Sun* reporter that he was working on an electric light, he had said it would be only a matter of days before his invention was ready for the marketplace. About a month later, in October 1878, the same reporter returned to Menlo Park. Edison showed him the latest version of his invention. It featured a thin, spiraled filament, or strand, made of platinum inside a small glass globe. When an electrical current was sent into the platinum filament, it glowed with light. The reporter described this marvel: "There was the light, clear, cold, and beautiful. The intense brightness [of the arc light] was gone. There was nothing irritating to the eye. The mechanism was so simple and perfect that it explained itself."[24]

But there was something that the reporter neglected to mention—the bulb could only burn for an hour. Edison's light was far from marketable, and he knew by then that perfecting his invention was going to take far longer than he had hoped. In a letter to a European associate, he admitted the troubles he was encountering with the light: "It has been just so in all my inventions. The first stop is an intuition, and comes with a burst, then difficulties arise—this thing gives out and then that—'Bugs'—as such little faults and difficulties are called—show themselves and months of intense watching, study and labor are requisite before commercial success—or failure—is certainly reached."[25]

These "bugs" were not the only challenges Edison was facing. He was under enormous pressure to work fast. He knew he had to solve the technical problems with his light quickly, or another inventor might beat him to the punch. And at the same time, Edison had to make sure enough money was coming in to pay his workers and keep his invention factory running.

PLEASING THE INVESTORS

In the past, Edison had always been welcoming to reporters. Because of that, many reporters were surprised, and a little taken back, when they arrived at Menlo Park and saw signs reading "Positively No Admittance." As Edison got deeper into the invention process, he became more reluctant to talk to the press. He wanted to tune out any distraction from the task at hand.

But there was one group of people whom Edison could not ignore—his investors. At first, Edison's lawyer, Grosvenor P. Lowrey, had easily found financiers willing to invest in the Edison Electric Light Company. After all, Edison was considered a genius, and he had already promised in print that he would design a working light in no time. For many investors, buying stock in his company seemed like a sure way to make a quick fortune.

However, when weeks passed and Edison was still hard at work, some investors began to get nervous. They heard rumors that another inventor, William Sawyer, was close to creating a

As Thomas Edison devoted more and more time to the invention of a practical electric light, he attempted to block out all distractions, including the press. Edison is pictured here around the time of his invention of the incandescent lightbulb.

functioning electric bulb using carbon, rather than platinum, for the filament. If Sawyer invented a workable light first, they could lose all the money they had invested in Edison's company. After learning that a few of the investors had a meeting with Sawyer, Edison became angry and upset; as his secretary explained in a letter to Lowrey: "He was visibly agitated and said it was the old story, i.e., lack of confidence. . . . All this he anticipated, but he had no fears of the result, knowing that the line he was developing was entirely original and out of the rut."[26]

UPTON JOINS THE TEAM

Growing more and more nervous, the board of directors of Edison's company asked him to hire an expert to help research the field of electric lighting. To please them, Edison agreed and hired Francis R. Upton. The young man had all the academic training Edison lacked, having studied mathematics and physics at Bowdoin College and Princeton University. Almost immediately, Upton became a valued member of Edison's inner circle at Menlo Park.

Before Upton's arrival, Edison's work on the electric light had been fairly haphazard, experimenting with one idea and then with another. But soon, Upton led Edison to a more methodical approach, with his own research helping to guide the experimentation. Edison found Upton to be a calming presence. Upton in turn respected the inventor's ingenuity. The two men would work closely together for 25 years.

While Upton researched existing patents, Edison began to study the gas lighting industry. He realized that if he was to create an effective electric lighting system, it would have to be better than the existing gas lighting system it would replace. Despite the problems with flames and fumes, most people were fairly satisfied with gas lighting. To make consumers switch, electric lighting would have to give them something extra. In addition to being safe and clean, Edison was convinced that electric lights had to be as cheap, if not cheaper, than gas lamps.

FILAMENTS AND GENERATORS

Looking to save money, Edison decided early on to use only thin strips of copper for his wiring, because copper was very expensive. This dictated several other important decisions: With wires this thin, he would have to use a low voltage electrical current. Voltage is the power that pushes electricity through wire. So, a low voltage could power an effective light only if the filament were made of a material with a high resistance to electrical energy.

With this in mind, Edison quickly decided that platinum would be the ideal material for the filament. But each decision he made came with a new set of problems. When the current heated up his platinum filament, the metal released gases that then caused the platinum to expand and crack. (This was the reason for the short life of the bulb Edison demonstrated for the *Sun* reporter in October 1878.)

Edison was also having trouble with his electrical generators. At first, he assumed he could buy manufactured generators to work with his lighting system. But as time passed, he concluded that he would have to build his own, tailor-made to work with the other parts of the system. His machinists worked hard, taking apart generators Edison bought, and then trying to rebuild them in a new way to meet Edison's changing needs.

After spending the last weeks of 1878 dealing with the generator problem without finding a solution, Edison returned to the question of the fragile filament. Still sure that platinum was the best material, he decided to change its environment. He placed the platinum in a glass bulb and pumped the air out of the space inside, creating a vacuum. In a vacuum, the metal did not break down as fast. Lucky for Edison, new devices for creating a vacuum had just come onto the market, making this process much easier than it would have been only months before. Still, making a vacuum required a good deal of work. In a notebook, Edison recorded, "We was all night bringing up 12 lamps in vacuum. Worked all day Sunday, all night Sunday night, all day Monday."[27]

DEMONSTRATING HIS PROGRESS

By the beginning of 1879, Edison had made some progress. But at the same time, his financial woes were growing. In January, he wrote Lowrey, "The fund I have here is very rapidly exhausted as it is very expensive experimenting."[28] Lowrey had done a masterful job of keeping the investors calm and happy. But he was wary of asking them for still more money without showing them proof that Edison's invention was coming along.

"A HIVE OF INDUSTRY"

By late 1878, Thomas Edison and his men were hard at work creating an electrical lighting system. In the January 17, 1879, edition of the *New York Herald*, a reporter recorded his impressions of Menlo Park. Traveling on the midnight express train, he found that, even in the middle of the night, the laboratory was alive with activity.

> The ordinary rules of industry seem to be reversed at Menlo Park. Edison and his numerous assistants turn night into day and day into night. At six o'clock in the evening the machinists and electricians assemble in the laboratory. Edison already present, attired in a suit of blue flannel, with hair uncombed and straggling over his eyes, a silk handkerchief around his neck, his hands and face somewhat begrimed and his whole air that of a man with a purpose and indifferent to everything save that purpose. By a quarter past six the quiet laboratory has become transformed into a hive of industry. . . . Every man seems to be engaged at something different from that occupying the attention of his fellow workman. Edison himself flies about, first to one bench, then to another, examining here, instructing there; at one place drawing out new-fancied designs, at another earnestly watching the progress of some experiment. Sometimes he hastily leaves the busy throng of workmen and for an hour or more is seen by no one. Where he is the general body of assistants do not know or ask, but his few principal men are aware that in a quiet

Although somewhat annoyed, Edison agreed to host a demonstration for the investors on March 26, 1879. He welcomed them into the new library at Menlo Park, richly decorated with cherrywood tables and chairs. For half an hour, Edison discussed his team's progress, promoting their efforts to find the

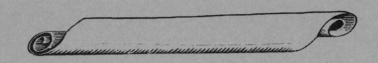

corner up stairs in the old workshop, with a single light to dispel the darkness around, sits the inventor, with pencil and paper, drawing, figuring, pondering. In these moments he is rarely disturbed. If any important questions of construction arise on which his advice is necessary, the workmen wait. Sometimes they wait for hours in idleness, but at the laboratory such idleness is considered far more profitable than any interference with the inventor while he is in the throes of invention. . . .

That Edison is in dead earnest in his work on the electric light is evidenced, among other ways, by the electrical appliances to be met everywhere in the laboratory. . . . Quantities of platinum and iridium for the incandescent light can be seen by the observer. Experiments of all sorts are nightly tried. All the well known magneto machines are carefully examined and experimented with, and their defects and advantages are immediately made known to Edison. . . .

As to the ultimate results of his work Edison seems more coherent than ever. The ominous predictions of those electricians and scientists who ridicule the idea of electricity supplanting gas seem to have only the effect of making him work till a later hour at night and order further quantities of platina and iridium.*

---

* "Edison Still Hard at Work in His Laboratory—His Latest Developments Concerning the Light," *New York Herald,* January 17, 1879.

perfect filament and generator. He then led his guests outside and took them to his machine shop. There, 12 electric lights illuminated the room, defying the cold, dark night outside.

The demonstration was a success. The investors were impressed enough to keep the money flowing into Menlo Park. Hoping to comfort Edison, Lowrey wrote, "They realize you are doing a man's work upon a great problem and they think you have got the jug by the handle with a reasonable probability of carrying it safely to the well and bringing it back full."[29]

SLOW WORK

At this point, though, Edison's jug was still far from full. However, in April, he had a significant breakthrough when his men created a generator that provided the cheap power Edison required. The gangly-looking device featured two five-foot-high magnets and weighed about 500 pounds. The crew gave it the nickname "Long-Legged Mary" (and later changed it to the slightly less suggestive "Long-Waisted Mary").

During the summer of 1879, Edison had to turn his attention to another business concern—marketing several telephonic devices in England. Work on the electric light ground to a halt. Upton was optimistic; although, in writing to his father, he expressed a weariness about their lack of progress: "The electric light goes on very slowly, I hope towards ultimate perfection. . . . We have not as yet what we want, but we have a good if not better [electric light] than anyone else in the world."[30]

Upton's assessment was fairly accurate. According to Edison scholars Robert Friedel and Paul Israel, in October 1879, "the Menlo Park lamp was much simpler and more elegant than it had been a year before. It consisted of a platinum spiral, containing only a few inches of wire, mounted in the middle of a sealed glass globe, exhausted to the best vacuum ever known."[31] But there was still one big problem—it just did not work. It could burn for only an hour or two before going dark.

SUCCESS WITH CARBON

Writing in the *New York Herald*, Edison's favorite reporter, Matthew Ferr, explained how the inventor finally solved this piece of the puzzle: "Sitting one night in his laboratory reflecting on some of the unfinished details, Edison began abstractedly rolling between his fingers a piece of compressed [carbonized—or turned into carbon by burning] lamp stick until it had become a slender filament. Happening to glance at it, the idea occurred to him that it might give good results as a burner if made incandescent. A few minutes later the experiment was tried, and to the inventor's gratification, satisfactory, although not surprising results were obtained. Further experiments were made, with altered forms and composition of the substance, each experiment demonstrating that at last the inventor was upon the right track."[32]

This tale of Edison's sudden flash of inspiration was typical of the romantic stories reporters liked to tell about the inventor. However, certainly by the fall of 1879, Edison's men were already trying to replace the platinum filament with a carbon one. Because heat can turn many substances into carbon, they tested a wide array of materials. But the most commonplace material of all—cotton thread—finally led to the breakthrough they were hoping for.

The experiment began in the early morning hours of October 21, 1879. Overseen by Charles Batchelor, the workers attached to a battery a bulb containing a horseshoe-shaped carbonized thread. When they turned on the current, the bulb glowed with a light equal to 30 candle flames. An hour passed, then another, and another. The bulb was still burning at dawn, then throughout the morning and into the afternoon. Finally, at about four o'clock, the bulb cracked and the light went out. It had burned for more than 13 hours.

Edison and his colleagues were thrilled. For the next few days, they spent long days in the laboratory, looking for an even better carbon filament. They methodically tried out all sorts of

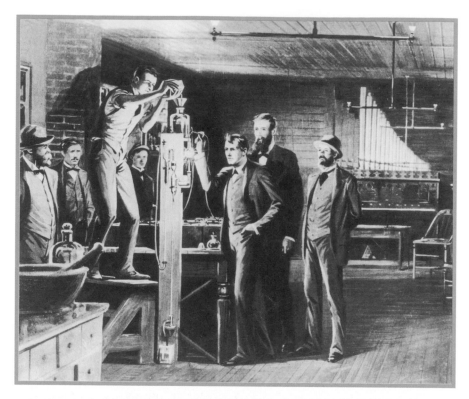

On the morning of October 21, 1879, Thomas Edison's Menlo Park scientists began an experiment that would lead to one of the most important scientific breakthroughs of the nineteenth century. By using a cotton thread to serve as the filament in their lightbulb, they were able to generate light for 13 hours. In this sketch of the birth of the incandescent light, Edison is depicted to the right of the lamp, while Charles Upton is immediately behind Edison, and Charles Batchelor is behind Edison and to his left. Francis Jahl is replenishing the mercury in the lamp.

other materials, including fish line and cotton soaked in tar. In a particularly festive moment, they decided to carbonize the beard hairs of two men working in the laboratory and hold a contest to see which would burn longest. Edison employee Francis Jehl later recalled, "Bets were placed with much gusto by the supporters of the two men, and many arguments held over the rival merits of their beards."[33] In the end, they settled on carbonized cardboard as the best filament material.

On November 2, Upton wrote his father about their progress: "The electric light is coming up. We have had a fine burner made of a piece of carbonized thread, which gave a light of two or three gas jets. Mr. Edison now proposes to give an exhibition of some lamps in actual operation. There is some talk if he can show a number of lamps of organizing a large company with three or five millions capital to push the matter through."[34] Two days after Upton wrote his letter, Edison applied for a patent for his new lightbulb.

SHOWING OFF THE LIGHT

With Edison's decision to publicly demonstrate his electric light system, Menlo Park became a flurry of activity. At the inventor's request, Western Union's president sent two linemen to string wires outside and inside two buildings Edison chose to light—Upton's home and the laboratory. His own workers struggled to construct enough bulbs, fuses, and fixtures in time for the demonstration, which Edison optimistically scheduled for New Year's Eve.

Edison kept reporters away, but news of what was happening at Menlo Park soon leaked out. Riders on the train line that passed through the village could see the laboratory glowing with light after the sun went down. As rumors spread, more and more passengers began riding the train just to catch a glimpse of the lights of Menlo Park. The line had to schedule extra trains to satisfy customer demand.

With the public desperate to learn more about his electric light, Edison decided to give an exclusive interview to the *Herald*'s Marshall Fox. In return, Fox agreed to let Upton edit his article. The piece filled more than a full page of the paper's Sunday edition on December 21, 1879. Celebrating the "Great Inventor's Triumph in Electric Illumination," Fox wrote, "Edison's electric light, incredible as it may appear, is produced from a tiny scrap of paper that a breath would blow away. Through this little strip of paper is passed an electric current, and the result is a great, beautiful light, like the mellow sunset of an Italian autumn. . . . And this light, the inventor claims, can be produced cheaper than that from the cheapest oil."[35]

Before his public demonstration, Edison scheduled a private one for his investors for December 27. The day before, investor Egisto Fabbri wrote Edison, reminding him of the importance of the event: "Any disappointment would be extremely damaging and probably more so than may appear to you as a scientific man."[36] Edison was fully aware that "any disappointment" would put the entire future of his invention in jeopardy. Bringing his lighting system to the market required a small fortune. Unless his lights wowed the investors, Edison was unlikely to get the monetary backing he needed. Even so, Edison was confident when welcoming the investors to the laboratory. The demonstration went off without a hitch, totally dispelling Fabbri's fears.

Four days later, Edison was ready to show his invention to the world. On that stormy winter night, more than 3,000 people arrived in Menlo Park. The crowd was a mix of invited guests in suits and gowns and curious local farmers still dressed in their work clothes. The *New York Herald* described the evening: "The laboratory was brilliantly illuminated with twenty-five electric lamps, the office and counting room with eight, and twenty others were distributed in the street leading to the depot and in some adjoining houses. The entire system was explained in detail by Edison and his assistants, and the light subjected to a variety of tests."[37]

The crowd was awed by Edison's achievement. But they were hardly surprised. After all, they had come to expect miracles from "The Wizard of Menlo Park."

Perfecting
the System

In the early weeks of 1880, curious crowds descended on Menlo Park each night, wanting to see Thomas Edison's amazing electric light for themselves. Pleased with his accomplishments, Edison often came out to greet them. He also enjoyed sifting through the bags of mail he received following his New Year's Eve demonstration. Some offered congratulations. Others proposed technical solutions to problems Edison was still encountering with the light. Many more were pleas for jobs from ambitious young men drawn to electricity, just as Edison had been only a decade before.

Among Edison's new admirers was Henry Villard. The president of the Oregon Railway and Navigation Company, Villard had attended the Menlo Park demonstration and came away impressed. He personally asked Edison to outfit the *Columbia*, a ship Villard was building, with its own electrical system. Edison had turned down many requests to light specific factories, stores, and public buildings. But given Villard's influence and wealth, Edison felt obliged to take on the project.

In April 1880, the *Columbia* was ready to set sail with its electric lighting system in place. The event set off another wave of adoring newspaper and magazine articles about Edison and his invention. *Scientific American* made a special mention of the superiority of electric lights over gaslights on a ship: "Certainly there is no place where a lamp of this character would be more desirable than on shipboard, where the apartments are necessary limited in size and pure air is a matter of great consequence."[38]

The lighting of the *Columbia* suggested that Edison could do well by focusing his business on specialty customers—such as shipbuilders and textile factory owners—whose businesses were most at risk for fire and the dark, gritty fumes of gaslights. But Edison had little interest in this kind of work. From the beginning, he wanted his invention used on the biggest scale possible, bringing light and electricity to as many American homes and businesses as he could.

THE BAMBOO FILAMENT

Edison had long before decided on his first step toward that goal—lighting a portion of the southern tip of Manhattan, which included the financial center of New York City. But he still had a long way to go before he could start on that project. Although impressive to visitors, the Menlo Park system did not yet work well enough for commercial use. Until he could improve the system, making it both more efficient and cost effective, Manhattan would have to wait.

Throughout 1880, Edison's employees worked long and hard, redesigning and testing every aspect of the system. Early on, they spent much of their energy perfecting the lightbulb. The carbon filament bulb they had created only burned for about 300 hours, far too short a time for a commercial bulb. Edison's patent on his carbon-filament bulb was also being challenged in court by inventor William Sawyer. Edison knew it would be far easier to get his system up and running if he evaded the court challenge by developing a new type of bulb.

A legend grew about how Edison came upon his new filament almost by accident. On a hot summer day in July 1880, Edison was cooling himself with a bamboo fan when he suddenly got an idea. He cut off a long piece of bamboo, carbonized it, and found it to be an excellent filament material. The story is probably not true, because laboratory records show that the Menlo Park engineers already had been considering bamboo for a while. In any case, by the summer, Edison was sure enough about the new material to send his associate William H. Moore on a trip to China and Japan in search of the best possible bamboo plant for their purposes.

UNDERGROUND WIRING

That summer, Edison also solved one of the most perplexing problems with his system. The wires he used to transmit electricity were made of pricey copper. Its use threatened to make the electric light more expensive than the gaslight, which would dash any hope of getting the number of customers he needed. Edison solved the problem by developing a new wiring system that cut the copper used to just one-eighth of what it had been before.

Edison was confident enough to schedule a demonstration of his new, improved system at Menlo Park for Christmas. But his staff continued to struggle with one particularly annoying obstacle: Edison wanted the system's wiring buried below the ground as it would be when installed in Manhattan. In the spring, once the ground had thawed, a crew began digging tunnels to hold the system's underground wires. It was an immense undertaking. Eight miles of wire had to be laid in order to light the 400 bulbs Edison envisioned.

In the summer of 1880, the Menlo Park engineers finally discovered the perfect material to use for the lightbulb's filament—bamboo. A bamboo-derived filament burned for more than 1,200 hours compared to just 300 hours for a carbon-derived filament.

At first, the project went well. But in July, after five miles were in place, a test showed there was a problem. The wire was improperly insulated and was not carrying a current. The men dug up the wire, insulated it again, and reburied it. Again, the system did not work. The wire had to be dug up and reburied ~~two more times before the system was ready. Finally at the~~ beginning of November, Edison was able to light up the streetlights of Menlo Park, illuminating the village's main road that connected the train station to Edison's compound. The system also lighted Edison's and Upton's own houses. Dazzled by the electric light, Upton's wife, Lizzy, approvingly wrote her sister, "The Electric Light is lovely now. I do wish you could see it."[39]

THE ALDERMEN'S VISIT

By December, Edison was ready to show off what he had done. Among the dignitaries he hosted were Sarah Bernhardt, a French actress who was an international celebrity. During a tour of the United States, she left New York for Menlo Park after one evening's performance. Arriving at two in the morning, she was welcomed by Edison, who through a translator explained his latest electrical innovations. Although she was thrilled by the lights of Menlo Park, Bernhardt was much more excited by Edison's phonograph. To her delight, the two took turns recording their voices—Bernhardt reciting French poetry and dramatic scenes, Edison singing "Yankee Doodle Dandy" and other American ditties.

As pleased as Edison was to meet the beautiful actress, he was soon playing host to visitors of far more importance to him and his future. If Edison's plan to light lower Manhattan was to move forward, he needed the permission of the New York City Board of Aldermen (members of the city legislature) to dig up the city's streets. Even if Edison got their OK, he was wary about what they might want in return. At the time, New York City officials were notoriously corrupt.

To try to get on their good side, Edison invited the aldermen to a private demonstration at his laboratory. With reporters in tow, they arrived in Menlo Park on the evening of December 20, 1880. As one reporter recounted, Edison enthusiastically greeted the aldermen, "grasp[ing] the hand of each one as he passed and smiled with all the frankness of a pleased school-boy."[40] He took them into his library and described his plan to light 51 blocks in lower Manhattan, assuring them that it would cost no more than gas lighting to the consumer. Edison went on, reminding them of his hundreds of patents and showing them the wonders of the phonograph. In the middle of his demonstration the aldermen became antsy. As one reporter explained, "[B]y this time the city fathers had

JOSEPH SWAN
(1828–1914)

The Inventor of an Early Electric Lightbulb

Arguably the inventor of the first workable carbon-filament lightbulb, Joseph Swan was born in England on October 31, 1828. He served as an apprentice to a druggist and then became a chemist in a company that made photographic plates. While there, he invented the dry-plate method of photography, which led to many more improvements in the field. In 1879, Swan was awarded a patent for bromide paper, still often used for photographic prints.

While in his twenties, Swan began to experiment with electrical lightbulbs. In 1860, he invented a bulb with a filament made of carbonized paper. His bulb, however, had some significant flaws. The filament, placed in an imperfect vacuum, could not withstand the heat of the current for long, and the batteries he used to power the bulb were expensive and unreliable.

Seventeen years passed before he returned to his invention. In those years, a new pump was invented that allowed him to create a better vacuum within his bulb. Also, Swan found, electrical begun to look quite dry and hungry, and as though refreshments would have looked much more palatable to them than the very scientific display"[41]

Edison was prepared. When his talk was over, the laboratory was turned into a dining room. A table offered a luxurious spread of turkey, duck, and ham, catered by Delmonico's, the most famous restaurant in New York at the time. With the champagne flowing, the aldermen seemed more and more enthusiastic about Edison's proposal. Echoing Edison's own

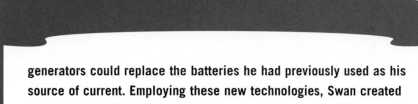

generators could replace the batteries he had previously used as his source of current. Employing these new technologies, Swan created an improved bulb, which he demonstrated in December 1878—11 months before Thomas Edison applied for a patent on his carbon-filament lightbulb.

Using his bulb, Swan wired his house, making it the first in England illuminated by electric light. In 1881, he formed a company to make and market his invention. Edison, however, soon challenged Swan in court, maintaining that the English inventor was infringing on his patent. Without the money or temperament for a lengthy legal battle, Swan decided to settle out of court. Together, Swan and Edison formed the United Electric Light Company in 1883.

The Englishman continued to work on improving his bulb. While looking for a better filament, he came upon a process that could produce artificial fibers. This process was later used to create the fabric now known as rayon.

In 1904, Swan was knighted for his contributions to chemistry and physics. Ten years later, on May 27, he died at the age of 86.

Shortly after Thomas Edison created a workable incandescent lightbulb, he turned his attention to lighting the streets of Menlo Park. In November 1880, Edison successfully illuminated the village's main road, from the train station to his home. Edison is pictured here with his first dynamo, which was responsible for generating light for Menlo Park.

words, one toasted the inventor, declaring, "Gas is dangerous. It is very easy for a man to go to his hotel, blow out the gas, and wake up dead in the morning. There is no danger of a man blowing out the electric light."[42]

The evening proved a success. Five months later, the aldermen granted Edison the right to dig up the streets of lower
Manhattan. The aldermen required Edison to repair any dam-
age to the streets and held his company financially responsible
for any destruction of property. In addition, the city would
charge the company five cents for each foot dug up, a fee so
low that the mayor objected. The only condition that worried
Edison was that he had to pay five inspectors $25 a week to
monitor the digging process. Edison was afraid they would
interfere with the work. But to his relief, the inspectors were
happy to show up once a week to collect their pay, never both-
ering to even glance at what Edison's crews were doing.

COMPETITORS EMERGE

The press reported on Edison's great success in wooing the
New York aldermen at Menlo Park, but at the same time, they
noted that Edison's lights were not the only game in town.
As the *New York Post* explained, "There are now six different
companies at work introducing electric lights in this city, the
lights being known as the Brush, Maxim, Edison, Jablochkoff,
Sawyer and Fuller [Gramme patents] lights."[43]

The Brush Electric Light Company was emerging as a particularly formidable competitor. Two days before Edison met
with the aldermen, the company's founder, Charles Francis
Brush, held a trial run of the first public electric lighting system in New York City. Powered by three generators, it used arc
lights to illuminate Broadway for the 22 blocks from 14th Street
to 36th Street. Brush's arc lights were far less technologically
advanced than Edison's incandescent bulbs, but neither the
press nor the public cared. They were wowed by the incredible
electric lights that seemed to turn night into day.

Hotels and theaters rushed to hire Brush to set up arc
lights. By the end of 1880, the company had erected about 55
in the city. After lighting Broadway for free for six months,
Brush signed a contract with the city to continue the service

Laying the Electrical Tubes.

During the spring of 1881, Thomas Edison was given permission to dig up the streets of lower Manhattan to wire the city for light. This illustration, which appeared in *Harper's Weekly* in June 1882, depicts this historic event.

and to set up lights in public areas such as Union Square and Madison Square as well. Edison had no doubt that his lighting system was superior to Brush's. Even so, Edison could see that in the race to light Manhattan, he would have to move faster if he was going to win.

Conquering Manhattan

By the beginning of 1881, Thomas Edison was ready to take on the Manhattan market. Lowrey, his lawyer, created the Edison Electric Illuminating Company in anticipation. But the great inventor still faced what he called "a stupendous obstacle"[44] before he could begin. He needed a large, steady supply of bulbs, generators, wires, and other assorted parts to set up his system for the commercial market. His investors, however, were unwilling to provide any more money to manufacture these necessary items. Edison had little choice: If he was to get his system up and running, he had to go into manufacturing himself, funding the endeavor with his own money. As he explained, "Since capital is timid, I will raise and supply [the needed money]. . . . The issue is factories or death!"[45]

He had already set up a lightbulb factory at Menlo Park under the direction of his trusted friend Upton. By the end of

1880, it was creating hundreds of bulbs a day. In early 1881, he extended his manufacturing empire by establishing Edison Electric Tube Company and Edison Machine Works. The bulb, tube, and machine factories were all funded by Edison and a few close associates.

WORKING AT "65"

By the spring, Edison was spending most of his time at his company's new Manhattan headquarters, nicknamed "65" after its street address, 65 Fifth Avenue. A mansion in the most fashionable neighborhood in the city, "65" had plenty of space for his growing staff, including engineers, draftsmen, electricians, and lawyers. Edison was proud of his elegant offices. He exclaimed, "We're up in the world now. I remember ten years ago—I had just come from Boston—I had to walk the streets of New York all night because I hadn't the price of a bed. And now think of it! I'm to occupy a whole house in Fifth Avenue."[46]

Edison moved his wife and children to a beautiful townhouse a few blocks away. But just as he had in Menlo Park, the inventor rarely spent any time at home. Consumed by his work, Edison could find little time for anything else, including his family.

Once "65" was up and running, Edison was able to focus on his next goal—wiring the area in southern Manhattan he called the First District. This 51-block district had been carefully chosen. He had sent out agents to interview the people who lived and worked there to determine their lighting wants and needs. His researchers found that the district was currently lit by some 20,000 gas jets and housed 1,500 potential customers, most of whom were willing to convert to electric light. These door-to-door interviews were invaluable to Edison's salesmen, who honed their sales pitch based on what people told them they wanted. The salesmen promised to wire customers for free and to provide electric lighting at about

In 1881, Thomas Edison moved the Edison Electric Light Company to a new address—65 Fifth Avenue in Manhattan. Edison is pictured here grasping the handrail on the left, with Charles Batchelor (center), and Major S. B. Eaton (right), the president of the company.

the same cost they were currently paying for gas lighting. The company also threw in a dozen free lightbulbs when a new customer signed up for electric service.

In the spring of 1881, Edison was ready to start wiring the First District. From the beginning, Edison was adamant about burying the wires underground. He was disturbed by what he called a "wilderness"[47] of electric wires hung from poles above American city streets. These overhead wires were put in place by an array of telegraph, telephone, and arc light companies. Because each company set up its own wiring, busy streets were hooded by a messy tangle of hundreds of wires. When a company went out of business, it usually did not bother to take down its wires. With everyday wear and tear, these abandoned wires often frayed, sometimes falling onto the street below and spraying passersby with sparks. Edison was determined that his lighting system would be safe, which meant burying his wires below city streets.

Teams of laborers began the hard work of digging trenches alongside the sidewalks of the First District. Each trench was about two feet deep. Inside they placed wires that had been wrapped in hemp and inserted into iron pipes. For further insulation, the pipes were filled with a mixture of hot paraffin and beeswax, which hardened as it cooled. Edison confidently stated that his insulated wires would last for 50 years—a prediction that would prove true.

THE PEARL STREET STATION

While the wires were being laid, Edison looked for a building to house the generators that would provide electricity for the First District. The location had to be in the middle of the district. Edison's system used a low voltage, direct current (current that travels in one direction). Direct current could not travel far, so his central power station had to be within one-half mile of every customer.

In May 1881, Edison found the perfect building for a cheap price in a run-down neighborhood. Located on Pearl Street, the large building had four stories and a basement. In the basement, Edison's company stored coal, which powered steam engines on the first floor. The steam in turn powered electricity-producing generators on the second floor. On the upper floors were banks of lamps used to test the system and measure the electricity the generators were creating.

Getting the Pearl Street Station up and running was tremendously difficult, as Edison later recalled: "It was a gigantic problem, with many ramifications. . . . All our apparatus, devices and parts were home-derived and home-made. Our men were completely new and without central station experience. What might happen on turning on a big current into the conductors under the streets of New York, no one could say."[48]

It was just as hard to say when the First District's lights would go on. Difficulties with the wiring, the generators, and other parts of the system caused delay after delay. By December, the press and the public were losing their patience with Edison's assurances. The *New York Times* reported, "Much grumbling has been done lately by businessmen and residents of the [First District] because there seems no prospect of the Edison Electric Light Company putting in the lights they promised to have burning by last November."[49] The paper further sniped that, while Edison's company had "laid a considerable quantity of wire . . . so far as lighting up the downtown district is concerned, they are as far away from that as ever."[50]

The criticism stung Edison, even though he had anticipated the public's impatience. As he once explained, "There is a wide difference between completing an invention and putting the manufactured article on the market. The public, especially the public of journalism, stubbornly refuse to recognize the difference. It was years after photography was invented before the first photograph was taken; years after the steamboat and telegraph were invented before they were actually set going. George Stephenson built his first locomotive ten years before he made his *Rocket* run from Liverpool to Manchester, and he and [steamboat inventor] Robert Fulton were called fool, charlatan, fraud, lunatic—everything they could think of. They demanded that he should 'hurry up,' or acknowledge himself a humbug."[51]

ELECTRIFYING MANSIONS

Despite the grumbling about delays, Edison and his workers trudged on. In the spring of 1882, the wiring started moving quickly as the cold ground thawed with warm weather. At the same time, however, Edison and some of his engineers became preoccupied by other projects, taking their attention away from the Pearl Street Station. In the fall of 1881, Edison had established the Edison Company for Isolated Lighting. This company installed isolated generators, which were used to light individual buildings, such as hotels, factories, and offices. Although a distraction from the development of the central power station, the isolated systems brought in a good deal of money. They also led Edison's engineers to develop many technological innovations that made their lighting system easier for customers to operate and for the Edison company to service.

But for Edison, the greatest advantage of the isolated systems was the attention they brought his company, especially from rich investors. For the wealthiest New Yorkers, a mansion wired for electricity became a new status symbol.

The first private residence Edison's company wired was that owned by William H. Vanderbilt. Having inherited $100 million from his father, railroad magnet Cornelius Vanderbilt, William H. Vanderbilt was the richest man in America. To show off his wealth, the younger Vanderbilt had a crew of 600 men spend two years constructing a 58-room mansion on Fifth Avenue. It was decorated with expensive furnishings from around the world, including fine art, bronze doors, and wallpaper adorned with jewels. Not surprisingly, Vanderbilt saw Edison's new invention as the perfect way to highlight his treasures.

By the spring of 1882, Vanderbilt's lighting system was ready. But when the lights were turned on, what should have been a moment of triumph for Edison turned into an embarrassment. The steam engine that powered the isolated generator made a tremendous amount of noise. As Edison later remembered, "Mrs. Vanderbilt became hysterical. . . . We told her we had a plant in the cellar, and when she learned we had a boiler there she said she would not occupy the house. She would not live over a boiler. We had to take the whole installation out."[52]

Edison had more luck with his next residential project. Investor J. Pierpont Morgan asked Edison to wire his Madison Avenue mansion. Wanting to stay in Morgan's good graces, Edison eagerly took on the job. By early 1882, the Morgan house was illuminated by 385 Edison bulbs. At first, Morgan was delighted with the system and started inviting friends and associates to his home for the sole purpose of showing it off. But the Morgan family soon learned the downside of living in the first house in New York lit by electric lamps. Their neighbors began complaining loudly as the engine and generators shook their houses. The engine also shot out smoky fumes into the street. At Morgan's insistence, Edison executive Edward H. Johnson eventually came to the house to personally upgrade the system. But the wires he placed under the floor short-circuited, setting Pierpont's library on fire.

LIGHTING THE FIRST DISTRICT

At the end of the summer of 1882, workers laid the last length of wiring in the First District. Edison's company then began hooking up building after building to the system. They also started secretly testing the lights they installed. Edison was nervous about publicly revealing the tests, knowing how many things could go wrong in a system that complex. But each successful test gave him more confidence. He began talking up his system in the press, emphasizing its advantages over gas lighting. Edison encouraged the public to exchange the "nauseous, dim flicker of gas, often subdued and debilitated by grim and uncleanly globes" for the electric light's "soft radiance. . . . [The electric light was] singularly powerful and even . . . perfectly steady."[53]

In early 1882, Thomas Edison illuminated financier and banker
J. Pierpont Morgan's (pictured here) Madison Avenue house with 385
lightbulbs. At the time, lighting a house was unwieldy, because the
steam engine responsible for powering the isolated generator was not
only very loud but also produced smoky fumes that polluted the air.

On September 4, 1882, Edison was finally ready to reveal what he had accomplished. He spent the morning at the Pearl Street Station, his shirtsleeves rolled up, tinkering until the last minute to make sure everything was perfect. In the early afternoon, he rushed to J. Pierpont Morgan's office in the financial firm of Drexel, Morgan & Company, where the board of directors for Edison's company had gathered. Then, Edison himself connected the lamps there to the circuitry of the main station.

LIGHTING THE TIMES BUILDING

Well aware of the power of the press, Thomas Edison wisely made it a priority to wire the office building of the *New York Times* as part of his Pearl Street Station project. Wiring the Times building ensured his lighting system in the First District would get attention from the newspaper. Also, because *Times* employees worked well into the night, it showed how useful his lighting system could be to other businesses that stayed open after dark.

On September 5, 1882, the day after Edison's successful demonstration of the Pearl Street central station, a *Times* reporter sang the praises of his new electric lamp, just as Edison had hoped.

> Yesterday for the first time The Times Building was illuminated by electricity. Mr. Edison had at last perfected his incandescent light, has put his machinery in order, and had started up his engines. . . . The lamp is simplicity itself. . . . The whole lamp looks so much like a gas-burner surmounted by a shade that nine people out of ten would not have known the rooms were lighted by electricity, except that the light was more brilliant than gas and a hundred

(Continues)

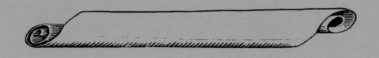

(Continued)

times steadier. To turn on the light nothing is required but to turn the thumbscrew; no matches are needed, no patent appliances. As soon as it is dark enough to need artificial light, you turn the thumbscrew and the light is there, with no nauseous smell, no flicker and no glare.

It was about 5 o'clock yesterday afternoon when the lights were put in operation. It was then broad daylight, and the light looked dim. It was not till about 7 o'clock, when it began to grow dark, that the electric light really made itself known and showed how bright and steady it is. Then the twenty-seven electric lamps in the editorial rooms, and the twenty-five lamps in the counting rooms made those departments as bright as day, but without any unpleasant glare. It was a light that a man could sit down under and write for hours without the consciousness of having any artificial light about him. There was a very slight amount of heat from each lamp, but not nearly as much as from a gas-burner—one fifteenth as much as from gas, the inventor says. The light was soft, mellow and grateful to the eye, and it seemed almost like writing by daylight, to have a light without a particle of flicker, and with scarcely any heat to make the head ache. . . . One night is a brief period in which to judge of the merits or demerits of a new system of lighting, but so far as it has been tested in the Times office, the Edison Electric Light has proved in every way satisfactory. When the composing rooms, the press rooms, and other parts of the Times building are provided with these lamps, there will be from 300 to 400 of them in operation in the building—enough to make every corner of it bright as day.*

---

* "Edison's Electric Light," *New York Times*, September 5, 1882.

Then, Edison, his associate Edward Johnson, and his investors all began watching the clock. At exactly 3 P.M., one of Edison's employees would turn on the main circuit breaker on Pearl Street. Then, one of two things would happen. The lamps in Morgan's office would either light up, signaling a stunning victory for Edison in the race to electrify America; or, the lamps would remain dark, indicating that Edison still had a long way to go to make his invention ready for the marketplace.

As they nervously waited, Johnson playfully suggested a wager. "One hundred dollars they don't go on!" he said to Edison. Without hesitation, Edison replied, "Taken!"[54]

At the strike of three, Edison won the bet. Just as planned, the interiors of buildings throughout about one-third of the First District were bathed in light. (The other two-thirds would be ready for illumination a few weeks later.) The *New York Tribune* declared Edison's system a success, noting, "Where the electric lights were in use last night the subscribers of the Edison Company expressed themselves gratified with their brief experience with the new illuminating agent."[55]

For Edison, the moment was the result of four hard, exhausting years of work. When interviewed by the *New York Sun,* he relayed his pleasure and relief with one simple statement: "I have accomplished all I promised."[56]

The War of the
Electric Currents

In the summer of 1884, 26-year-old Nikola Tesla negotiated
his way through the crowded streets of New York City. He was
headed to Thomas Edison's headquarters at 65 Fifth Avenue.
Tesla carried with him a letter from Edison's old friend and
associate Charles Batchelor, who was promoting Edison's
inventions in Europe. Like many people in European scientific circles, Batchelor recognized Tesla as an extremely well-
educated and talented electrical inventor.

Many years later, Tesla recalled his introduction to Edison
at 65: "The meeting with Edison was a memorable event in
my life. I was amazed at this wonderful man who, without
early advantages and scientific training, had accomplished
so much."[57]

At the time of their meeting, two years after the successful
Pearl Street Station start-up, Edison was feeling frustrated with

his accomplishments in the field of electric lighting. Edison was expanding his lighting business quickly, but he was still having trouble selling his central stations. To make a profit, his salesmen had to convince hundreds of customers within a small area to sign on for his electric service. By the end of 1884, Edison's company had installed only 18 central stations in the United States.

DEATH AND MARRIAGE

That year, Edison also suffered a great personal blow. Working into the wee hours of August 9, he received a telegram that his 29-year-old wife, Mary, had died. She had suffered for years from a number of ailments, both physical and mental. Edison's daughter Dottie later remembered waking up that morning to see her father kneeling at Mary's bedside, "shaking with grief, weeping and sobbing."[58]

Unsurprisingly, Edison dealt with his grief by throwing himself into his work. Yet he knew that as a workaholic widower with three children to raise, he needed to remarry as soon as possible. That winter, he attended the World Industrial and Cotton Centennial in New Orleans, where he ran into Lewis Miller, a rich industrialist from Ohio. With Miller was his attractive, lively 19-year-old daughter, Mina. At the time, Mina was engaged to the son of a preacher. Lewis Miller, though, hoped that Mina would marry someone with greater wealth and social standing. Edison certainly seemed to fit the bill.

With Lewis's blessing, Edison courted Mina. The couple married on February 22, 1885. Two months before, they had toured the wealthy suburb of Llewellyn Park in West Orange, New Jersey. There, Edison purchased Glenmont, an enormous mansion on a hill, which he presented as a gift to his bride-to-be.

THE WEST ORANGE LABORATORY

Near his mansion, Edison constructed a new laboratory. Built under Charles Batchelor's supervision, the huge complex
(continues on page 73)

NIKOLA TESLA
(1856–1943)

A Visionary Inventor
in the Field of Electricity

A genius and visionary, Nikola Tesla was perhaps the most inno-
vative scientist working at the dawn of the electric age. Born in
Croatia on July 10, 1856, Tesla showed a tremendous grasp of
mathematics and science even as a small boy. After graduating
from high school, he traveled to Graz, Austria, in 1875. He studied electricity there and began experimenting with alternating
current.

Tesla worked briefly at a telegraph office in Budapest,
Hungary, before landing a job at the Continental Edison Company
in Paris. Working as a troubleshooter at Edison plants in France
and Germany, he attracted the attention of Thomas Edison's trusted associate Charles Batchelor. In 1884, Batchelor sent Tesla to
work for Edison in New York. He gave Tesla a letter addressed to
Edison that read, "I know two great men and you are one of them;
the other is this young man."[*]

For a year, Tesla designed generators and motors for the
Edison Machine Works. But Tesla was frustrated by Edison's
direct current system. He recommended that Edison start using
alternating current—a suggestion the inventor did not appreciate,
given his enormous investment of time and money into direct current. After a dispute over pay, Tesla left the company and formed
his own.

Devoting all his time to experimenting with alternating current, Tesla acquired more than 40 patents by 1891. His most
important invention was a motor that employed alternating current. Businessman George Westinghouse bought Tesla's patent
for this device and hired him to work on the AC system he was
developing. In large part due to Tesla's work, Westinghouse's

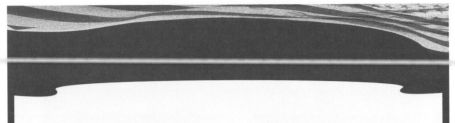

system eventually beat out Edison's as the most popular electrical system in the world. Tesla became famous, but because of the terms of his deal with Westinghouse, he saw far less money from his invention than he deserved.

By the mid-1890s, Tesla was studying the wireless transmissions of radio waves. Italian inventor Guglielmo Marconi was credited with inventing the wireless radio. But many scientists contended that Tesla was more entitled to this honor because of his own early work in the field.

After 1900, Tesla struggled in both his life and his work. With little money, he had trouble performing the experiments he envisioned. Tesla also became increasingly eccentric. Living alone in a New York City hotel, he developed a host of odd phobias. He came up with many bizarre theories. Tesla claimed he could pick up radio waves from intelligent life on Venus and Mars. He also said he had the capacity to build a death beam that could destroy America's enemies.

Despite his peculiarities, Tesla received many honors from his peers, including the Edison Medal of the American Institute of Electrical Engineers in 1917. When he died in 1943, more than 2,000 people attended his funeral, and U.S. President Franklin Roosevelt sent a testimonial to celebrate Tesla's achievements. Since his death, many scientists, including several Nobel laureates, have expressed their great debt to Tesla. His work is said to have anticipated a wide array of later inventions, including the electron microscope, the television, the microwave oven, and the computer.

---

* Stephen S. Hall, "Tesla: A Scientific Saint, Wizard, or Carnival Sideman?" *Smithsonian*, June 1986.

In 1884, Thomas Edison's first wife, Mary, died. Edison dealt with his grief by throwing himself into his work, but he had three young children to raise, so he set out to find a new wife. While attending the World Industrial and Cotton Centennial in New Orleans that winter, he met Mina Miller (pictured here), the daughter of a rich industrialist from Ohio, and the couple were married a year later.

(continued from page 69)

would eventually grow to be 10 times the size of Menlo Park. In addition to the main building, the complex included separate structures housing a machine shop, a glassblowing shop, an electrical testing center, and a chemistry laboratory. Stocking the laboratory with some 8,000 chemicals, Edison joked that he had "ordered everything from an elephant's hide to the eyeballs of a United States Senator."[59]

Edison had high hopes for his West Orange laboratory: "I will have the best-equipped and largest facility extant [in existence], incomparably superior to any other for rapid and cheap development of an invention, and working it up into commercial patterns with models, patterns, and special machinery. . . . I expect to turn out a vast number of useful inventions and appliances in industry. . . . In time, I think it would grow into a great industrial work with thousands of men."[60]

After years of trying to market his electric light system, Edison was eager to focus on inventing again. He explored improvements in telegraphy and telephony and continued to work on his phonograph. He also dabbled in many side projects, including creating a cotton picker and developing an artificial alternative to silk.

One of his oddest obsessions at West Orange was the talking doll. Edison was convinced the invention would be a moneymaker. At the time, American parents indulged their daughters with expensive porcelain dolls from Europe, which cost as much as $30 apiece. Edison figured that a talking doll could fetch at least that much. He devoted an entire building at West Orange to manufacturing the talking doll, with the hope of eventually producing 500 a day. His doll, however, was a disappointment in the marketplace. Initial enthusiasm for the toy faded after it was clear the delicate phonograph device inside inevitably broke during shipping.

RIVALS AT WORK

While Edison was working in the lab, his lighting empire was presented with a new threat. George Westinghouse, a business-man who had made a fortune by inventing a braking system for railroads, began buying up patents in the electrical lighting field. He became convinced that he could develop a lighting system superior to Edison's.

Westinghouse recognized that Edison's system had one great flaw: It relied on low-voltage direct current (DC), which could only travel in one direction for a short distance. The system, therefore, only made economic sense in urban areas with a very dense population. In less-populated areas, there were too few customers for an Edison central station to make a profit.

Westinghouse imagined a system that instead used high-voltage alternating current (AC)—that is, current that flowed in two directions. AC current could travel for many miles, so a power station could service customers spread out over a large area.

At first, Edison dismissed Westinghouse's company. He joked that Westinghouse should "stick to air brakes."[61] But Edison could not ignore his new rival for long. By the end of 1886, Westinghouse's first year in business, he had built 68 AC central stations, making him Edison's biggest competitor. Charles Coffin, another of Edison's rivals, had also embraced alternating current. Coffin operated the Thomson-Houston Company. Originally focusing on arc lighting, Thomson-Houston also began constructing AC stations.

DISMISSING AC

For many of Edison's employees, one thing quickly became clear—AC was superior to DC in powering electric lighting systems. Among those employees was Nikola Tesla. He met with Edison to suggest that the great inventor embrace AC. According to Tesla, Edison replied "very bluntly that he was not interested in alternating current; there was no future to it and anyone who dabbled in that field was wasting his time; and besides, it was a deadly current whereas direct current was safe."[62] Tesla soon left Edison's company and later went to work for Westinghouse.

Edison executive Edward Johnson also made the case for AC, telling Edison that by sticking to DC he was ensuring that "we will do no small town business, or even much headway in cities of minor size."[63] Upton also tried to get Edison to convert to AC.

Why was Edison so reluctant to shift from DC to AC? His conviction that high-voltage AC was potentially deadly was certainly part of the reason. But his pride also played a role. Edison had helped to design just about every element of his DC system and, understandably, was fiercely proud of what he had done. Despite the obvious advantages of AC, he simply could not admit to himself, much less to anyone else, that there could be a better system than his own.

A KILLING CURRENT

By 1887, Edison was devoting much of his energy to one goal—discrediting Westinghouse and his alternating current system. His company's annual report laid out his case against AC, dismissing it "from a commercial standpoint, having no merit in itself and, being of high pressure . . . notoriously destructive of both life and property."[64]

Late that year, out of the blue, Edison received a letter from Alfred Southwick, one of three members of the New York State Death Commission. The commission was charged with finding a new way of executing prisoners sentenced to death. In the past, the state had hanged condemned prisoners. But in a few highly publicized hangings, prisoners had died slow, horrible deaths because of an executioner's incompetence. New York now wanted an execution technique that would kill instantly and painlessly.

One of Thomas Edison's chief rivals was George Westinghouse, who is pictured here in 1868. Westinghouse made his fortune by developing a braking system for railroads, but in the 1880s, he set out to develop a better lighting system than Edison's.

Southwick thought death by electrocution was the solution. He wrote to Edison, asking his thoughts on the matter. Edison quickly replied: He had nothing to say because he did not believe in capital punishment. Southwick wrote again, insisting that Edison had a duty to society to help him. "Science and civilization demand some more humane method than the rope," he declared. "The rope is a relic of barbarism and should be relegated to the past."[65]

Again, Edison wrote back, this time saying he had changed his mind about helping Southwick. Edison offered him some advice: "The most effective of those are known as 'alternating machines,' manufactured principally in this country by Geo. Westinghouse. . . . The passage of the current from these machines through the human body even by the slightest contacts, produces instantaneous death."[66] After some consideration, Edison had realized that the ideal means of attacking Westinghouse had just fallen into his lap. If he could persuade New York State to execute prisoners with AC, he could make Westinghouse's system forever connected with death in the public mind.

WARNING!

In February 1888, Edison enthusiastically upped the stakes in what had become known as the "War of the Electric Currents." He published an 84-page booklet, not-so-subtly titled "WARNING!" In its first half, Edison attacked companies that he felt were intruding on his lightbulb patents. For several years, Edison had employed an army of lawyers to go after what he called "patent pirates."[67] In the second half of the booklet, Edison let loose his rage against Westinghouse. He charged that Westinghouse's system was too expensive and dangerous. Even worse, he claimed that Westinghouse knew his current could kill but did not care, just as long as he could make some money from it.

In June, Edison's side in the "war" got a little unexpected help. The *New York Evening Post* published a controversial article, "Death in the Wires," by an electrical engineer named Harold Brown. The piece echoed Edison's charges against Westinghouse. Brown wrote: "Several companies who have more regard for the almighty dollar than for the safety of the public, have adopted the 'alternating' current for incandescent service. If the pulsating [arc] current is 'dangerous,' then the 'alternating' current can be described by no adjective less forcible than *damnable*."[68] Brown also offered a solution to the problem. He proposed outlawing the use of current of more than 300 volts, which would effectively put Westinghouse out of business. (There is no evidence that Edison himself had anything to do with Brown's article, but the *Post* was in fact owned by one of his investors.)

The article caught the attention of the New York City Board of Electrical Control. The board requested that Brown appear at a meeting and read his article. The board also asked Westinghouse to write a response, but at first he declined. Instead, he wrote to Edison directly. Diplomatically, Westinghouse blamed the recent war of words not on Edison, but on "some people [who want] to do a great deal of mischief and create as great a difference as possible between the Edison Company and The Westinghouse Electric Co., when there ought to be an entirely different condition of affairs."[69] Westinghouse invited Edison to his house to work out their differences. Edison sharply declined, saying he was too busy to make the trip.

When his effort at peacemaking failed, Westinghouse decided to abandon diplomacy. He wrote the New York City Board of Electrical Control, declaring the attacks against him were "unmanly, discredible and untruthful."[70] Other AC experts sent letters questioning Brown's credentials and competence.

A SHOCKING DEMONSTRATION

Brown became determined to protect his professional reputation. Edison was just as determined to help him. The inventor offered Brown access to the West Orange lab to develop an experiment to prove just how deadly AC could be.

In July 1888, Brown was ready to demonstrate his findings to the electrical control board. Before the board members and a group of reporters, Brown explained that he would show that living beings were far more likely to survive a shock from direct current than from alternating current. He left the room and returned with a black retriever. Brown placed the dog in a cage with copper wires wrapped between the bars. With his assistant's help, he attached the wires to two of the dog's legs.

Brown then sent 300 volts of DC through the wires. The dog looked shaken. Brown upped the current to 400 volts. The dog yelped and tried to escape. At 700 volts, it thrashed around, and at 1,000 volts, the dog let out hideous yelps. Finally, Brown zapped the poor animal with 330 volts of AC, and it immediately fell dead.

By this time, the crowd was yelling for him to stop. As one reporter wrote, "Many of the spectators left the room, unable to endure the revolting exhibition."[71] Brown tried to explain how he had proven that AC was the deadlier current, but no one wanted to listen. To a chorus of jeers, Brown left the room, prematurely ending the demonstration.

But Brown was hardly ready to give up. With Edison's support, he lobbied to have the New York State Death Commission adopt death by AC as its official method of execution. In December, two members of the commission, along with several reporters and influential scientists, were invited to West Orange for another demonstration at Edison's lab. Edison himself attended, making the occasion even more newsworthy.

This time, Brown sent alternating current through several animal subjects, slaughtering first a calf and then a horse. Instead of responding with revulsion, the committee members were impressed by AC's capacity to kill. They agreed that from then on state executions would be carried out by shocks of alternating current, and they hired Brown to develop an appropriate device. Through the gruesome demonstration, Edison had succeeded in winning a central battle in his war with Westinghouse.

"Electric Lights
Are Too Old
for Me"

The year 1889 presented Thomas Edison with plenty of good news. Even as the war between DC and AC raged, Edison's reputation still attracted plenty of new investors. That spring, his old friend and financier Henry Villard proposed that Edison unite his seven companies, with the support of bankers in Germany and the United States. The result was a massive new company, the Edison General Electric Company.

In the fall, Edison traveled to Paris with his wife, Mina, to attend the Universal Exhibition there. The leading attraction at the great fair was the newly constructed Eiffel Tower. But many visitors also flocked to the Gallery of Machines, where Edison General Electric showed off its wares in a display that covered nearly an acre. As usual, Edison himself made news, charming the international press and public with his down-to-earth manner.

EXPOSITION UNIVERSELLE — LE PHONOGRAPHE
(Aquarelle inédite de Antigus).

In the fall of 1889, Thomas Edison traveled to Paris for the Universal Exposition, where he displayed many of his inventions. Edison is depicted here demonstrating his phonograph, which he invented in 1877.

When he returned to the United States, Edison was met with still more good fortune. In October, the U.S. Circuit Court in Pittsburgh decided in Edison's favor over the four-year patent dispute. To Edison's great satisfaction, the judge in the case declared, "But for this discovery electric lighting would never have become a fact."[72]

CRUEL AND UNUSUAL?

In 1889, a gruesome news story out of Buffalo, New York, even seemed to play to Edison's advantage. While in a drunken rage, a Buffalo man named William Kemmler murdered his girlfriend with an axe. After a four-day trial, Kemmler was sentenced to death. With death by electrocution now the official means of execution in New York State, Kemmler was to be the first criminal to die from alternating current. Kemmler's death, Edison hoped, might also spell the end of Westinghouse's AC empire.

But before the execution could take place, Kemmler's lawyer, former New York congressman William Bourke Cockran, appealed the case. Cockran did not argue that Kemmler was innocent. He claimed the sentence of death by execution was in violation of the U.S. Constitution, because it amounted to cruel and unusual punishment. Cockran maintained there was no guarantee that an electric current would kill quickly or painlessly. As part of his evidence, he cited Harold Brown's dog-killing demonstration of the previous year. As one member of the electrical board testified, "It was one of the most frightful scenes I have ever witnessed. The dogs writhed and squirmed and gave vent to their agony in howls and piteous wails."[73]

Edison had been hesitant to get too directly involved in the campaign for AC executions, preferring Brown to serve as his mouthpiece. But, fearing Cockran would win the appeal, he agreed to testify before the court. Cockran asked Edison, "In your judgment, can artificial electric current be generated and applied in such a way to produce death on human beings in every case?"[74] Edison immediately answered with a simple "yes." That was enough for the press to turn against Cockran. A reporter for the *Albany Journal* wrote, "The Kemmler case at last has an expert that knows something concerning electricity. Mr. Edison is probably the best informed man in America, if not the world, regarding electric currents and their destructive powers."[75]

DEATH BY ALTERNATING CURRENT

Kemmler lost his appeal, but Cockran took his case to a higher court. Newspapers dutifully reported on the proceedings while covering every detail about Kemmler's life in jail in Albany, New York. At the same time, Edison executives tried to come up with ways to make the most of the upcoming execution. They even attempted to coin a new verb—to "westinghouse," meaning to die by electrocution.

Finally, on August 6, 1890, the wait was over. His appeals exhausted, Kemmler was led into a room outfitted with a large oak armchair—the electric chair Harold Brown developed to deliver the fatal current. As Kemmler sat down, thick leather straps were tied around his wrists and ankles to hold them in place. A cloth hood was placed over his head. Seats for about 25 witnesses, including two reporters, were arranged in a horseshoe in front of Kemmler.

As the execution began, the witnesses could hear the click of a switch, which started up the generator in a room nearby. Kemmler's body jolted forward. The New York Times reported that he was "as rigid as though cast in bronze, save for the index finger of the right hand, which closed up so tightly that the nail penetrated the flesh on the first joint and the blood trickled out on the arm of the chair."[76] After 17 seconds, the prison doctor declared that Kemmler was dead, and the generator was turned off.

Then a witness shouted, "Good God! He is alive!"[77] All looked to see Kemmler's chest heaving up and down in frantic breaths. A prison official rushed to turn the generator back on, and in a few moments, the room was filled with a horrible smell of charred meat. The electric chair had roasted Kemmler's body. Nearly all the witnesses were nauseated by the smell. One reporter fainted, while the county sheriff began to cry.

Under the headline "Far Worse Than Hanging; Kemmler's Death Proves an Awful Spectacle," the New York Times printed every disgusting detail of the execution. Edison was quoted as saying, "I have merely glanced over an account of Kemmler's death and it was not pleasant reading."[78] He tried to blame the doctor for the whole affair, but too many people remembered Edison's promises that the electric chair would deliver a fast and humane death. While hoping to destroy Westinghouse, Edison had only tarnished his own reputation. Asked to comment on the execution, Westinghouse quite rightly said, "It has

GEORGE WESTINGHOUSE
(1846–1914)

Thomas Edison's Chief Competitor

As both an inventor and businessman, George Westinghouse made extraordinary contributions to U.S. industry during the late nineteenth century. Born on October 6, 1846, Westinghouse was raised in New York State, where his father worked as a farmer and carpenter. When George was 10, the family moved to the town of Schenectady, New York. There, his father established a machine shop, George Westinghouse & Company. Working in the shop, young George quickly gained an understanding of the workings of machinery, and he began inventing his own.

After serving in the Union Navy during the Civil War (1861–1865), George Westinghouse briefly studied engineering at Schenectady's Union College. But after he acquired his first patent, Westinghouse quit school to become a full-time inventor. After working on train machinery for several years, he made his first great invention—a new air brake system for slowing down trains. In 1869, he became president of the Westinghouse Air Brake Company.

Westinghouse next devoted himself to creating an improved system for sending natural gas through pipes. In the course of his work,

been a brutal affair. They could have done it better with an axe
. . . . The public will lay the blame where it belongs and it will
not be on us."[79]

A COMPANY MERGER

With the botched Kemmler execution, Edison's war to dis-
credit Westinghouse came to an end. At the same time, his

he began studying the new field of electric lighting. Westinghouse
became convinced that alternating current could deliver electricity
more efficiently and at less cost than the direct current upon which
Thomas Edison's lighting system relied. In 1886, Westinghouse
established the Westinghouse Electric Company to compete directly
with Edison. Among the patents Westinghouse purchased to develop
his new system was one for an alternating current motor invented by
Nikola Tesla. The motor allowed Westinghouse to provide customers
with not only electric lighting, but also electric power for appliances
and other machines.

The success of Westinghouse's alternating current system made
him extraordinarily wealthy. By the beginning of the twentieth century, Westinghouse had established nine companies in the United
States and five in Europe. Together they were worth about $120 mil-
lion. However, due to a sudden downturn in profits, Westinghouse
was forced to give up control of the Westinghouse Electric Company
in 1911.

In his final years, he suffered from ill health and was confined to
a wheelchair. When George Westinghouse died on March 12, 1914,
he was honored as one of the greatest industrialists in U.S. history.

company was in trouble. As Westinghouse happily pointed out in an article in the *North American Review,* electric light customers preferred AC to DC by five to one. By 1891, investors were reacting by selling off Edison General Electric stock, which made the company's stock price plummet.

Edison's financiers were also worried about the company's profitability. In 1891, Edison General Electric had sales of $11 million and made $1.4 million in profit. For the same year, its competitor Thomson-Houston had sales of $10 million and made $2.7 million in profit. In other words, with nearly the same amount of sales, Thomson-Houston made about double the profits of Edison General Electric. To Edison investor J. Pierpont Morgan, this statistic meant one thing—Edison General Electric was being mismanaged.

On February 5, 1892, Morgan met with Henry Villard, the president of Edison General Electric, and Charles Coffin, the president of Thomson-Houston. He negotiated a merger between the two firms. Doubtful of Villard's talents as a manager, Morgan arranged for Coffin to become president of the new company, which was called General Electric.

GOOD-BYE TO THE ELECTRIC LIGHT

In New York, a journalist friend of Edison's secretary, Alfred O. Tate, told Tate about the merger. He was shocked. He had had no idea what Morgan had been planning. Worse, Tate was sure Edison knew nothing about it, either.

Tate rushed out to West Orange to deliver the news to his boss. Edison was just as stunned as Tate had been. Tate later wrote, "I never before had seen him change color. His complexion naturally was pale, a clear healthy paleness, but following my announcement it turned as white as his collar."[80]

In some ways, the merger was good news for Edison. He came out of the deal $2 million richer. Edison had been eager to spend more of his time in the laboratory, and the money would allow him to develop some of his latest inventions and ideas.

Thanks largely to its declining profits, Edison General Electric was forced to merge with Thomson-Houston Electric Company of Lynn, Massachusetts, in 1892. Pictured here is the interior of Thomson-Houston's plant in 1888, four years prior to the merger.

But the merger dealt a deep personal insult to Edison in a very public way. Morgan had not bothered to consult him about the negotiations. Just as disturbing, the new company dropped "Edison" from its name. As Tate explained, "His pride had been wounded. . . . And that name had been violated, torn from the title of the great industry created by his genius through years of intensive planning and unremitting toil."[81]

Edison tried to conceal his bitterness, adopting a cocky attitude with the press. He declared he was out of the electrical lighting industry and happy about it. As he told one reporter, "I cannot waste my time over electric-lighting matters, for they are old. I ceased to worry over those things ten years ago, and I have a lot more new material on which to work. Electric lights are too old for me."[82]

THE IRON ORE EXTRACTOR

General Electric thrived and remains today one of the largest companies in the world. But true to his word, Edison, after the merger, all but gave up on the electric lighting industry. He returned to West Orange, where he initially threw all his energy into a pet project he had been toying with for years—inventing a machine to extract iron ore, the material used to make steel.

By the 1890s, most of the iron ore mines in the eastern United States were considered used up, forcing the steel industry to rely on new mines in the West. Edison, however, believed that he could make the eastern mines active again. They still contained rock with traces of iron ore, but the ore was too hard to get out with existing mining technology. To solve the problem, Edison envisioned a device that would crush the rock, and then extract the ore from the rubble using a giant magnet. With characteristic confidence, he predicted that "with this perfect process I will have a monopoly of one of the most valuable sources of national wealth in the U.S."[83]

Reluctant to rely on investors ever again, he used his own money to buy 19,000 acres of New Jersey land and establish a rock-crushing plant in the town of Ogden. The venture proved to be a money sink. By the time Edison closed the plant in 1900, he had lost his fortune. At least to the press, Edison voiced no regrets: "I never felt better in my life than during the five years I worked here. Hard work, nothing to divert my thoughts, clear air, [and] simple food made life very pleasant."[84]

Due to a number of failed ventures in the 1890s, including a failed attempt to invent a profitable iron ore extractor, Thomas Edison's fortune had largely disappeared by the turn of the twentieth century. Undaunted, Edison returned to his laboratory and continued to create important new inventions.

EDISON'S LATER TRIUMPHS

Edison returned to the laboratory, spending the rest of his life inventing. He and his employees developed an astounding array of devices. With the help of an excellent team of lawyers, Edison was able to secure 1,093 patents in his name.

Several of Edison's later inventions had almost as much impact on American life and culture as the electric light. Improvements to Edison's early crude phonograph produced a device that could record and play back music, which eventually made the modern music industry possible. He also secured patents on the most important technologies in the early motion picture industry. Edison was a pioneer in film history, producing many of the first short movies. He was the mastermind behind the influential *Great Train Robbery,* the first feature to show how motion pictures could tell a complete story.

In his later years, Edison had regained his lost fortune and then some, accumulating riches of about $12 million. Still courted by the press, he was regarded as a great American hero, so much so that his birthday was celebrated almost like a national holiday. His friend Henry Ford, himself famed for innovations in the young automobile industry, paid Edison a special honor in the 1920s by reconstructing the Menlo Park laboratory as part of Ford's Edison Institute (now the Henry Ford Museum and Greenfield Village) in Dearborn, Michigan.

The institute was dedicated on October 21, 1929—the fiftieth anniversary of Edison's invention of the lightbulb. Before an elite audience that included Nobel Prize–winning scientist Marie Curie and aviation pioneer Orville Wright, Edison himself reenacted the moment of invention. Despite all his later accomplishments, in the public mind he was still celebrated as the man who gave the world the electric light.

The Electric Age

Two years after his appearance at Henry Ford's Edison Institute, Thomas Edison died on October 18, 1931, at the age of 84. For two days and two nights, more than 50,000 mourners came to view his body, which was laid in the library at his West Orange laboratory. Further evidence of Edison's fame and stature came from a tribute decreed by President Herbert Hoover: He asked Americans to commemorate Edison by dimming their lights for one minute on the night of the great inventor's funeral.

Unsurprisingly, Edison's death was well covered in the press, with many lengthy articles trumpeting the highlights of his career. They hailed him as the "Conqueror of the Unknown" and the "Genius of Light."[85] The *St. Louis Post* went so far as to say, "If we had a mythology, Mr. Edison would be placed in [the] gallery of gods."[86] Edison's obituaries inevitably listed a number of the more than 1,000 inventions patented in his name. But nearly all agreed with the *New York Times* obituary in declaring his "lamp [that] ended [the] 'dark ages'" as "his greatest work."[87]

In fact, Edison's light has had an astounding impact. Nearly every aspect of American life has been in some way transformed because of this invention. Whether in the public square, the workplace, or the home, electric light and electric power have helped to define the world we know today.

WELL-LIT STREETS

For financial reasons, electric companies first concentrated on selling their service to local governments and businesses. Cities were especially interested in investing in street lighting. The wiring required many workers, so by installing electric lights, city officials could generate plenty of jobs for their communities.

The public also embraced street lighting. Having streets lit at night made people feel safer. Outdoor lights not only reduced street crime—they also helped keep vehicles from crashing into each other on the street and pedestrians from tripping and falling on sidewalks. Real estate owners also encouraged city officials to install streetlights, because they could increase the value of their properties.

The first streetlights appeared in the country's largest urban centers. But by the late 1890s, General Electric and Westinghouse began marketing their services to smaller cities. Between 1900 and 1920, most cities installed streetlights—not just because they were practical, but also they were considered a symbol of their communities' prosperity. Often, cities held parades—complete with floats, bands, and speeches—to celebrate their new streetlight system.

A CHANGING CITYSCAPE

By the beginning of the twentieth century, streetlights were not the only thing illuminating American cities. Businesses discovered that lighted signs were an effective way of promoting their wares. New York's Broadway became especially well known for its electric signs, earning the street the nickname "the Great White Way." Many New Yorkers enjoyed the new signs, which included one erected by H. J. Heinz featuring a 45-foot-long pickle made from green lightbulbs. Some condemned the signs as vulgar eyesores, destroying the beauty of the city. The pickle sign prompted one commentator to complain that "the dancing flash light of the 57 varieties of beans, pickles, etc. [is] thrown in the faces of all who throng Madison Square."[88]

Broadway also became famous for another type of sign— the marquee. The theaters that lined the street used electric signs to promote their shows and stars. Soon, having one's "name in lights" became synonymous with success as a performer. Electric lights also allowed for new types of nighttime entertainments, such as ball games played in lighted sports stadiums.

The wiring of New York and other cities also dramatically changed their skylines. Elevators operated by electricity allowed for the construction of tall skyscrapers. The electric light also gave architects more freedom in designing large buildings, because they no longer had to rely on the sun as their only source of interior light. At night, the exteriors of skyscrapers were often lit up as well, creating a glamorous array of lights against the dark sky. Dramatically lit nighttime skylines of U.S. cities attracted tourists and inspired artists. In words and images, they celebrated city skylines as symbolic of everything modern in the twentieth-century United States.

TRANSPORTATION TRANSFORMED

Another electrical innovation that changed U.S. city life was the streetcar. Long before Edison began work on the electric light, inventors had tried to create large electric cars that could transport passengers through city streets. But they relied on

(continues on page 96)

"THE DREAM OF THE INCANDESCENT LAMP"

For journalists across the country and around the world, the death of Thomas Edison provided an occasion to evaluate his illustrious career. On October 18, 1931, a *New York Times* reporter offered his contribution to these tributes. As shown in the following excerpts, the *Times* obituary, like most others, celebrated the electric light as the shining glory of Edison's legacy:

> Thomas Alva Edison made the world a better place in which to live. . . . No one in the long roll of those who have benefited humanity has done more to make existence easy and comfortable. . . .

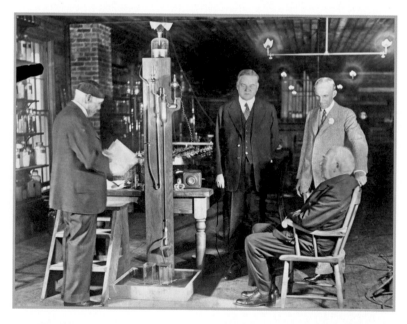

In 1929, Thomas Edison and his friend Francis Jehl reenacted the initial illumination of the incandescent lightbulb as part of the fiftieth anniversary of the occasion and to mark the opening of Edison's Menlo Park lab in Henry Ford's Greenfield Village, Michigan, museum. Pictured here left to right are Jehl, President Herbert Hoover, Ford, and Edison.

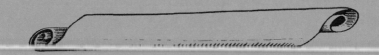

His inventive genius brooded over a world which at nightfall was engulfed in darkness, pierced only by the feeble beams of kerosene lamps, by gas lights or, in some of the larger cities, by the uncertainties of the old-time arc lights. To Edison, with the dream of the incandescent lamp in his mind, it seemed that people still lived in the Dark Ages. But his ferreting fingers groped in the darkness until they evoked the glow that told him the incandescent lamp was a success, and that light for all had been achieved. That significant moment occurred more than fifty years ago—on Oct. 21, 1879.

A blustering wind beat gustily on the unpainted boards of a small laboratory in Menlo Park, N.J. A tall, lean figure stooped over a shaky table, his steel-blue eyes filled with the impassioned light of discovery. Beside him was a thin, nervous assistant. The dull golden glow of kerosene lamps, puffing off an oily odor, cast grotesque shadows on the walls, as every chance gust of air down the lamp chimneys twisted the erratic flame. . . .

The two men in the laboratory were looking from a dim present into a dazzling future, from darkness to Broadway's brightest display. Gravely Francis Jehl told Mr. Edison that the lamp on the table had a good vacuum. An organ pump in a corner was started to force the air from the lamp. A minute or two went by in breathless silence. Then the inventor tested the vacuum. It was right, and he told Jehl to seal the lamp. The great moment was at hand. They moved to the dynamo and started it. Light sprang from the lamp like a newly created world to the watching men. Edison put on more power. He thought the makeshift filament would burst. Instead it grew bright. More power and more light. At last it broke. But the incandescent lamp had been invented.*

---

* Thomas Edison Obituary, *New York Times* On Line Learning Network. Available online at *http://www.nytimes.com/learning/general/onthisday/bday/0211.html*

(continued from page 93)

expensive power from batteries that constantly required recharging. Streetcars only became practical and economical once they could be powered by generators housed in large central stations like those Edison pioneered.

Before streetcars, people traveled through city streets on foot or in horse-drawn wagons and carts. These vehicles could not carry very many people, so streets were always clogged with slow-moving traffic. Streets were also covered with horse manure, making cities smelly and unsanitary.

Not surprisingly, city dwellers quickly embraced electric streetcars. They left streets cleaner and could travel at higher speeds than horses. The cars could also plow through snow and climb steep hills. Outfitted with electric lights and heaters, they provided customers with a fairly comfortable ride, too.

In addition, streetcars changed the way people lived. Because downtown areas were easier to get to by streetcar, they became business and shopping centers. Large department stores, some as big as a city block, opened up, offering shoppers a greater variety of goods than they had ever seen before. Shop windows were lit up with electric lights to highlight the stores' wares, encouraging people to participate in the country's growing consumer culture.

Streetcars also allowed people to easily travel outside the city. As streetcar lines expanded outward, many decided to live in more rural areas and commute to the city for work. These outlying communities became known as suburbs. By the 1930s, except in some large cities, most streetcars were no longer in operation. They had been replaced by automobiles as people's preferred mode of transportation. But suburbs still remained popular, with commuters now using their cars to drive to work.

MECHANIZED WORK

Like local governments, businesses immediately saw a financial incentive to install electric lighting. In fact, by 1900, factories consumed more than half of all electrical power used in the United States. Both factory owners and workers benefited from electric lights. By lighting factories before dawn and after dusk, owners could extend the hours their businesses operated and therefore earn larger profits. By laboring under electric lights rather than gaslights, workers enjoyed a safer and cleaner work environment. Also, in factories with machines that performed very meticulous work, electric lights helped workers better see what they were doing.

After 1890, more and more factories began to use electric power in addition to electric light. Electricity could power machines that did a wide variety of work. As factory work became run more by machines than people, owners could hire less skilled laborers. This drove down the cost of their wages. In part because of the electrification of the factory, between 1890 and 1940, America's productivity—the amount of work needed to produce a good or service—rose by 300 percent.

For many workers, however, the news was not so good. Electricity caused their wages to fall and their workdays to grow longer. It was common to work in an assembly line, a method pioneered by automobile manufacturer Henry Ford in the 1910s. On Ford's assembly line, a worker used a machine to perform just one small task, usually taking less than a minute. Using assembly lines, Ford reduced the amount of time needed to make a car from 12 hours to 1.5 hours. But for the laborer, working on an assembly line was often incredibly boring and depressing. To make a living, many proud, skilled workers were forced to take jobs that required no skills and left them with little pride.

ELECTRICITY IN THE HOME

In the early twentieth century, few private homes were wired for electricity. In 1907, only 8 percent of houses in America had electric lights. However, as the cost of electricity dropped,

In cities, powering streetcars was one of the most important early uses of electricity. Streetcars were powered by batteries that often had to be recharged. The generators that Edison developed to power his electric light made it practical and economical for streetcars to replace wagons and carts in America's cities.

that number rose quickly. By the 1930s, most American houses in or near cities were wired.

Houses gradually changed after the introduction of electricity. Homes built for gas-lamp lighting had many small rooms. If a gas flame made one room stuffy, residents could open a window and close the door to allow the room to air out. With electric lighting, this was no longer necessary, so houses could have more open floor plans. Homeowners also began demanding large porches. Well-lit by electric lights, porches would serve as dining areas on hot summer nights.

Electricity also changed home décor. In gaslit homes, dark-colored furniture, rugs, and curtains hid the grime produced by gas lamps. Once homes were wired for electricity, people felt free to decorate rooms using lighter, brighter colors.

A WORLD OF APPLIANCES

For city dwellers accustomed to gas lamps, electric lighting did not really alter their day-to-day activities. Electric appliances, however, did. In fact, over time, these devices dramatically altered everyday life.

Even before their homes were wired for electricity, most American families were familiar with little electric gadgets that ran on batteries. They might have played with electric toy trains, or decorated their Christmas trees with strands of electric lights. But by about 1920, Americans could purchase an array of new items powered by motors that ran on the electric current transmitted into their homes. These appliances included electric irons, washing machines, heating pads, toasters, and vacuums. These products were extremely exciting to Americans. Once they became available for purchase, most people who still had gas lighting got their houses wired just so they could use these appliances.

Advertising campaigns and door-to-door salesmen encouraged people to try out these new marvels. Because many appliances were used in housecleaning, they were often marketed specifically to women. In *Good Housekeeping* magazine, Edison himself touted that the "Woman of the Future" would no longer be a "domestic laborer" but instead a "domestic engineer . . . with the greatest of all handmaidens, electricity, at her service."[89] Electric appliances, the advertisements claimed, were timesaving devices that would free women from household drudgery and allow them to devote their time to grander pursuits.

As it turned out, housewives ended up spending about the same amount of time cleaning as they had before the advent of these fabulous new appliances. This was largely because the standards of cleanliness rose. For example, in the past, women may have cleaned their rugs by beating out the dirt four times during the year. But once vacuums became commonplace, they likely used them once per week. Also, in the age of appliances, fewer middle-class women could expect household help from their husbands or from paid servants.

ELECTRIFYING RURAL AMERICA

Electric lights and early electric appliances had a much greater impact on Americans living in rural areas. Electricity came late to American farms. Companies did not want to wire isolated rural communities because there were too few customers to justify the expense. In 1930, about half of all Americans lived on farms. But only about one in every nine farms had electricity.

The situation changed only after the federal government stepped in. During the mid-1930s, U.S. president Franklin D. Roosevelt initiated a set of policies called the New Deal, which were designed to help provide employment for the many Americans out of work during the Great Depression. One of his New Deal policies was the Rural Electrification Administration (REA). Its goal was to build transmission lines to bring electricity to farms across the United States. Roosevelt maintained that the government had a moral responsibility to electrify rural areas. As he explained, "Cold figures do not measure the human importance of electric power in our present social order. Electricity is no longer a luxury, it is a definite necessity."[90]

Within just a few years, farm families gave up candles and oil lamps in favor of electric lights. These forever changed the rhythm of farm life. The farmer's day had been dictated solely by the rise and fall of the sun. Now the farmer could labor before sunrise and after sunset, adding hours to each workday and lending him more flexibility with his time than ever before.

During the Great Depression, much of rural America was electrified thanks to President Franklin Roosevelt's Rural Electrification Administration (REA). By 1939, the federal program served 288,000 households, which translated to approximately a quarter of the rural homes in the country.

NEW MACHINES ON THE FARM

Like factories, farms also became much more productive because of electricity. Farmers soon had access to an array of machines that helped them with their chores. Everything from electric milking machines to electric corn shelling machines made a farmer's work easier and less time-consuming. For the individual farmer, these machines were a blessing. But for the farming industry as a whole, they made farms so productive that fewer were needed to supply the nation with food and other farm goods. As a result, electricity put some farmers out of business.

The farmhouse also experienced great changes. Farm families invested in the same types of domestic appliances bought by city dwellers. They also installed electric water pumps, allowing them to have indoor plumbing. Unlike urban women, farm wives found that such conveniences substantially cut down the time and energy they devoted to household chores. Electric washing machines, for instance, greatly simplified the task of washing clothes. In the past, women had to pump water from wells and then scrub each piece of clothing separately on a washboard—a chore that was both time-consuming and physically exhausting.

The appliance most valued by farm families, however, was the radio. Living in remote areas, people on farms often had to travel great distances to reach a small town or to visit a neighbor. Radios helped relieve their sense of isolation. For the first time, with just the turn of a knob, they could hear news from around the country and even around the world.

The modern conveniences that electricity brought to rural areas made those regions more attractive to nonfarmers. People who wanted to live in a more natural setting could now move to the country without giving up the comforts of household appliances and indoor plumbing. The electrification of rural areas, therefore, allowed their populations to rise.

MODERN ELECTRICAL MIRACLES

By the mid-twentieth century, electric lighting was commonplace just about everywhere in the country. Many appliances had become a part of everyday life as well. But during the decades since, new electrical inventions have continued to reshape U.S. society.

One of the most important was the air conditioner. Just as electric lights disrupted humankind's age-old sense of daytime and nighttime, air-conditioning made the change of seasons much less important in determining people's activities. With central heating and cooling systems readily installed in homes and businesses, the season or climate of the area in which people live has a relatively small effect on their daily lives. Air-conditioning has been especially important in the southeastern and southwestern United States. Freed from the consequences of stifling heat, the "Sun Belt" has enjoyed substantial economic and population growth in recent decades.

Another electrical device that changed the United States was the television. Today, television—and related devices such as DVDs, videotape players, and video game consoles—offers Americans a huge array of entertainment options available to them around the clock. Similarly, the concept behind Edison's phonograph has evolved into the CD and the MP3 player, which now provide consumers with nonstop musical entertainment.

Widely available electricity has also made possible some incredible communication tools, such as the rechargeable cell phone and e-mail. The Internet, too, has transformed daily life by allowing immediate access to an enormous amount of information.

ELECTRICITY AND OUR WORLD

Of course, these marvels have not come without a price. In the social arena, television and computers have often led to physical and psychological isolation. For some, life viewed on a screen has somehow become more real than the world out-side. In economic terms, the dawn of the Internet and related technologies have sped up the growth of the global economy, which now threatens the livelihoods of many less skilled American workers. And from an environmental perspec-tive, the production of electricity from burning coal pollutes the air and worsens global warming, placing the earth itself in jeopardy.

There is one simple way of solving these problems brought about by society's embrace of electricity: People could stop using electric light and electric power. But, of course, that idea is absurd. Regardless of what troubles society's reliance on electricity creates, the benefits it has given society are much greater. In fact, it is nearly impossible to imagine life in the modern United States without the gifts electricity has given us. In that sense, Thomas Edison deserves the place of reverence he still holds in American culture as one of the country's greatest inventors. With every flick of a light switch, one can witness how his intelligence, determination, and imagination helped reshape lives.

CHRONOLOGY

1847 Thomas Alva Edison is born in Milan, Ohio, on February 11.

1863 Edison begins working as a telegraph operator.

1868 Edison is granted his first of 1,093 patents for his electronic vote recorder.

1869 Edison becomes a full-time inventor.

1876 Edison establishes an invention factory in Menlo Park, New Jersey.

1877 Edison invents the early phonograph.

1878 **September** Edison announces his intention to invent the electric light.

October 16 The Edison Electric Light Company is established.

1879 **November 4** Edison applies for his first lightbulb patent.

December 31 Edison hosts a public demonstration of his electric lighting system in Menlo Park.

1880 Edison establishes his company headquarters at 65 Fifth Avenue in New York City.

1882 Edison's first permanent power station opens on New York's Pearl Street in September.

1887 Edison builds an expanded laboratory in West Orange, New Jersey.

1888 Edison launches the "War of the Electric Currents" against rival George Westinghouse.

1889 The Edison General Electric Company is established.

1890 Edison is derided for his support of the electric chair after the execution of William Kemmler.

1892 Edison General Electric merges with the Thomson-Houston Company to form General Electric; Edison vows to end his work on electric lighting.

1893 Edison begins commercial production of motion pictures.

1896 Edison introduces the first phonograph for the home market.

1900 Edison gives up on his iron ore extraction business.

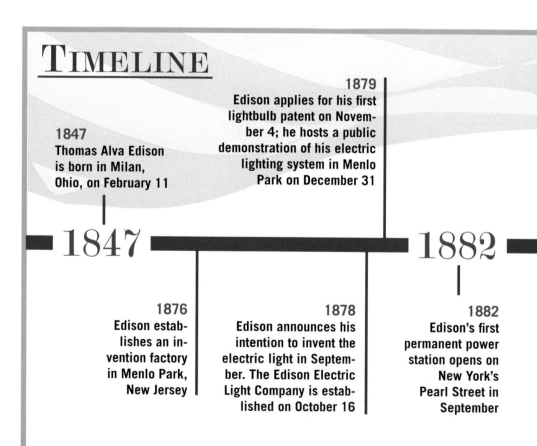

TIMELINE

1879
Edison applies for his first lightbulb patent on November 4; he hosts a public demonstration of his electric lighting system in Menlo Park on December 31

1847
Thomas Alva Edison is born in Milan, Ohio, on February 11

1847

1882

1876
Edison establishes an invention factory in Menlo Park, New Jersey

1878
Edison announces his intention to invent the electric light in September. The Edison Electric Light Company is established on October 16

1882
Edison's first permanent power station opens on New York's Pearl Street in September

1929   Edison participates in a reenactment of the invention
        of the electric light in Dearborn, Michigan.

1931   Thomas Edison dies on October 18; Americans dim
        electric lights for one minute to commemorate Edison
        on the day of his funeral.

1888
Edison launches
the "War of
Electric Currents"
against rival
George
Westinghouse

1929
Edison par-
ticipates in a
reenactment of
the invention of
the electric light
in Dearborn,
Michigan

1887
1931

1887
Edison builds
an expanded
laboratory in
West Orange,
New Jersey

1892
Edison General
Electric merges with
the Thomson-Houston
Company to form Gen-
eral Electric; Edison
vows to end his work
on electric lighting

1931
Thomas Edison
dies on October
18; Americans dim
electric lights for
one minute to com-
memorate Edison
on the day of his
funeral

NOTES

CHAPTER 1

1. "Edison's Newest Marvel. Sending Cheap Light, Heat, and Power by Electricity," *New York Sun* (September 16, 1878).
2. Ibid.
3. Ibid.
4. Ibid.
5. Jill Jonnes, *Empires of Light: Edison, Tesla, Westinghouse, and the Race to Electrify the World* (New York: Random House, 2003), 45.
6. Ibid., 48.
7. Ibid.
8. Robert Friedel and Paul Israel, *Edison's Electric Light: Biography of an Invention* (New Brunswick, N.J.: Rutgers University Press, 1987), 8.
9. "Edison's Newest Marvel," *New York Sun.*
10. Ibid.
11. Jonnes, 58.

CHAPTER 2

12. Neil Baldwin, *Edison: Inventing the Century* (New York: Hyperion Books, 1995), 24.
13. Paul Israel, *Edison: A Life of Invention* (New York: John Wiley & Sons, 1998), 7.

CHAPTER 3

14. Baldwin, 47.
15. Ibid., 56.
16. Ibid., 61.
17. Ibid., 89.
18. Friedel, 33.
19. Baldwin, 71.

20. Ibid., 81.
21. Ibid.
22. Ibid., 90.
23. Jonnes, 104.

CHAPTER 4

24. Friedel, 26.
25. Ibid., 28.
26. Ibid., 26.
27. Ibid., 78.
28. Jonnes, 60–61.
29. Friedel, 39.
30. Baldwin, 111.
31. Friedel, 88.
32. Ibid., 94.
33. Jonnes, 63.
34. Friedel, 104.
35. Jonnes, 65.
36. Ibid.
37. Ibid., 66.

CHAPTER 5

38. Friedel, 143.
39. Ibid., 183.
40. Jonnes, 74.
41. Ibid.
42. Ibid.
43. Ibid., 75.

CHAPTER 6

44. Ibid., 76.
45. Ibid.
46. Ibid., 77.
47. Baldwin, 135.
48. Jonnes, 81.
49. Ibid., 82.
50. Ibid.
51. Baldwin, 116.
52. Jonnes, 13.

53. Baldwin, 137.
54. Jonnes, 84.
55. "Electricity Instead of Gas,"
    New York Tribune, September 5,
    1882.
56. Ibid., 85.

CHAPTER 7

57. Ibid., 105.
58. Baldwin, 143.
59. Jonnes, 171.
60. Baldwin, 183.
61. Jonnes, 151.
62. Ibid., 107.
63. Ibid., 142.
64. Ibid.
65. Ibid., 149.
66. Ibid.
67. Ibid., 150.
68. Ibid., 165.
69. Ibid., 167.
70. Ibid., 168.
71. Ibid., 172.

CHAPTER 8

72. Ibid., 179.
73. Ibid., 193.

74. Ibid., 194.
75. Ibid., 196.
76. Ibid., 211.
77. Ibid., 212.
78. Ibid., 213.
79. Ibid.
80. Ibid., 240.
81. Ibid., 244.
82. Ibid., 242–243.
83. Ibid., 348.
84. Ibid., 350.

CHAPTER 9

85. Baldwin, 209.
86. Ibid.
87. Thomas Edison Obituary,
    New York Times On Line Learn-
    ing Network. Available online at
    *http://www.nytimes.com/learning/
    general/onthisday/bday/0211.html*
88. David E. Nye, *Electrifying
    America: Social Meanings of
    a New Technology, 1880–1940*
    (Cambridge, Mass.: The MIT
    Press), 5.
89. Nye, 242.
90. Ibid., 304.

BIBLIOGRAPHY

Baldwin, Neil. *Edison: Inventing the Century.* New York: Hyperion Books, 1995.

Collins, Matthew, producer. *Edison's Miracle of Light.* Video-tape, 60 min., 1995. Newton, N.J.: Shanachie Home Video.

Friedel, Robert, and Paul Israel, with Bernard S. Finn. *Edison's Electric Light: Biography of an Invention.* New Brunswick, N.J.: Rutgers University Press, 1987.

Israel, Paul. *Edison: A Life of Invention.* New York: John Wiley & Sons, 1998.

Jonnes, Jill. *Empires of Light: Edison, Tesla, Westinghouse, and the Race to Electrify the World.* New York: Random House, 2003.

Lighting a Revolution. National Museum of American History. Available online at *http://americanhistory.si.edu/lighting/index.htm.*

Nye, David E. *Electrifying America: Social Meanings of a New Technology.* Cambridge, Mass.: MIT Press, 1990.

The Thomas A. Edison Papers. Available online at *http://edison.rutgers.edu.*

FURTHER READING

BOOKS

Adair, Gene. *Thomas Alva Edison: Inventing the Electric Age.* New York: Oxford University Press, 1996.

Collier, James Lincoln. *Electricity and the Light Bulb.* New York: Benchmark Books, 2005.

Jonnes, Jill. *Empires of Light: Edison, Tesla, Westinghouse, and the Race to Electrify the World.* New York: Random House, 2003.

Levinson, Nancy Smiler. *Thomas Alva Edison: Great Inventor.* New York: Scholastic, 1996.

VIDEOTAPES

Collins, Matthew, producer. *Edison's Miracle of Light.* Video-tape, 60 min., 1995. Newton, N.J.: Shanachie Home Video.

WEB SITES

Lighting a Revolution. National Museum of American History

http://americanhistory.si.edu/lighting/index.htm

Drawing on an exhibition at the Smithsonian's National Museum of American History, this site discusses electric lighting inventions of the nineteenth and twentieth centuries.

The Thomas A. Edison Papers

http://edison.rutgers.edu

The Edison Papers project of New Jersey's Rutgers University has catalogued more than 5 million documents relating to Edison's life and work. Its Web site includes a searchable database of about 180,000 documents in digital format.

Thomas A. Edison and the Menlo Park Laboratory—The Henry Ford Museum

http://www.hfmgv.org/exhibits/edison

This Web site offers several essays and a chronology of Edison's life, times, and work.

Edisonia. National Park Service

http://www.nps.gov/edis/edisonia.htm

This Web site includes recordings, movies, photographs, and other resources from the Edison National Historical Site.

Edison's Miracle of Light. PBS American Experience

http://www.pbs.org/wgbh/amex/edison

Associated with the PBS documentary "Edison's Miracle of Light," this Web site offers biographical information about Edison, a timeline of his life and work, and photographs and recordings relating to his long career.

PICTURE CREDITS

INDEX

About the Author

LIZ SONNEBORN is a writer, living in Brooklyn, New York. A graduate of Swarthmore College, she has written more than 50 books for children and adults, including *Guglielmo Marconi: Inventor of Wireless Technology*, *The American West*, *A to Z of American Indian Women*, and *The New York Public Library's Amazing Native American History*, winner of a 2000 Parents' Choice Award.